Working with Elder Abuse

of related interest

The Abuse of Older People
A Training Manual for Detection and Prevention, 2nd edition
Jacki Pritchard
ISBN 1 85302 305 1

Good Practice in Supervision
Statutory and Voluntary Organisations
Edited by Jacki Pritchard
ISBN 1 85302 279 9
Good Practice 2

Good Practice in Risk Assessment and Risk Management
Edited by Jacki Pritchard and Hazel Kemshall
ISBN 1 85302 338 8
Good Practice 3

Good Practice in Child Protection
A Manual for Professionals
Edited by Hilary Owen and Jacki Pritchard
ISBN 1 85302 205 5
Good Practice 1

Hearing the Voice of People with Dementia
Opportunites and Obstacles
Malcom Goldsmith
ISBN 1 85302 406 6

Abuse, Neglect, and Expoitation of Older Persons
Strategies for Assessment and Intervention
Edited by Lorin A Baumhover and S Colleen Beall
ISBN 1 85302 405 8

Developing Services for Older People and their Families
Edited by Rosemary Bland
ISBN 1 85302 290 X
Research Highlights in Social Work 29

Reviewing Care Management for Older People
Edited by Judith Phillips and Bridget Penhale
ISBN 1 85302 317 5

Working with Elder Abuse

A Training Manual for Home Care, Residential and Day Care Staff

Jacki Pritchard

Jessica Kingsley Publishers
London and Bristol, Pennsylvania

The right of Jacki Pritchard to be identified as author of this work has been asserted by her in accordance with the Copyright, Designs and Patents Act 1988.

First published in the United Kingdom in 1996 by
Jessica Kingsley Publishers Ltd
116 Pentonville Road
London N1 9JB, England
and
1900 Frost Road, Suite 101
Bristol, PA 19007, U S A

Copyright © 1996 Jacki Pritchard

Library of Congress Cataloging in Publication Data
A CIP catalogue record for this book is available from the Library of Congress

British Library Cataloguing in Publication Data
Pritchard, Jacki
Working with elder abuse : a training manual for home care,
residential and day care staff
1. Aged – Abuse of 2. Aged – Care
I. Title
362.6

ISBN 1-85302-418-X

Printed and Bound in Great Britain by
Athenaeum Press, Gateshead, Tyne and Wear

Contents

The following symbols have been used throughout the book for ease of recognition:

case examples

handouts

exercises

case studies

simulation exercises

role play

For my son Nathan who has been as patient and tolerant
as ever whilst I have been working on this book

Acknowledgements

I would like to thank all the home care and residential/day care staff I have met and worked with during the past six years. They inspired me to get this book written and I could not have done so if they had not been willing to share their experiences with me.

I would also like to express my appreciation to all those local authorities where I have trained these two groups of staff. Particular thanks are due to Mike Oldham, Training Officer, and other staff who work for Wakefield Social Services; also to Sue Fenton and Janet Blackburn, Training Officers, and all the residential staff in Calderdale Social Services.

Introduction

Since I first started providing workshops and courses on elder abuse, I have trained many different people – both professionals and non-professionals – in different work settings. My own working experiences have changed and developed since I first became interested in elder abuse back in the 1980s. I first worked as a social worker and then became a manager in area offices but also in hospital settings. My last post within a social services department was as a Locality Manager which involved managing social workers, home care staff and a residential unit. So my experience of elder abuse in the community and in institutions has broadened over the years and I believe I have a good understanding of how elder abuse affects not only victims and abusers, but also people working with cases of abuse.

What has become painfully clear to me is that home care staff and staff working in residential units and day centres are crucial people in identifying abuse. This is because they have more face-to-face contact with clients than maybe a social worker does, they spend more time with clients and get to know them better and, crucially, they may have access to an older person's body because they dress/undress, wash/bath them and so on.

Unfortunately, it is these two groups of staff who may not be seen as a priority for training in this area of work. Also, when they report suspected abuse they are often not listened to, not taken seriously or ignored completely (because 'what do they know? They are not professionals'!).

I felt I had to write a training manual specifically for these staff groups. My objective is that the book can be used by individual teams/staff groups to facilitate their own development in working with elder abuse. My original book *The Abuse of Elderly People* (Pritchard 1992) was designed so that anyone working with older people would begin to think about elder abuse. It was just a beginning, although I believe that the exercises are still very valuable for *all* professionals, and this current manual should be used in conjunction with the second edition, *The Abuse of Older People* (Pritchard 1995). My hope is that if training sections cannot provide the necessary number of courses for home care and residential/day care staff then the information, materials and exercises which follow can be used in staff meetings, development meetings and (individual or group) supervision sessions.

HOW TO USE THE MANUAL

The manual has been designed so that training officers can use it as a training package or managers can systematically work through it with their teams. When time is short and precious, I think it is also possible to dip into the manual and use bits of it to look at certain problems as they arise for workers. The chapters contain a mixture of theory, exercises and a suggested reading list.

The theory is written simply so that it can be used to present information in training sessions, and handouts are presented within the text. The exercises and materials are presented within each chapter, but Chapters 11 and 12 consist of role plays and case studies which can be used as additional material for exercises.

I do not expect workers to read vast amounts of articles and books, but the suggested reading lists are at the end of each chapter for people who are organizing training sessions and might want to read around a subject/issue area in more depth. As I stated above, this manual should be used in conjunction with *The Abuse of Older People*; the appropriate references are given in this text.

I have devoted two chapters to residential and day care issues. Home care staff should also use these chapters because some of their clients may be abused when they go into hospital or when they go into a unit for respite care or at a day centre. So home care staff need to think about what abuse could take place in an institution.

TERMINOLOGY

We all have different ways of saying things; and I hate to admit it but we all use jargon as well. I had to think very carefully about which words I was going to use within the manual. So it might be useful to list some of the terms I use commonly in the manual:

client	a person with whom home care, residential or day care staff work
resident	a person living in a local authority home or private sector home
day centre user	a person who attends day centre
victim	a person who has been abused
abuser	a person who has engaged in any abusive act
worker	this can refer to any home care, residential or day care staff
trainer	training officer, manager of homecare staff, manager of residential/day care staff

REFERENCES

Pritchard, J. (1992) *The Abuse of Elderly People: A Manual for Professionals*. London: Jessica Kingsley.

Pritchard, J. (1995) *The Abuse of Older People*, 2nd edition. London: Jessica Kingsley.

1 Elder Abuse – What is it?

It is very important for all workers to be clear in their own minds what abuse means to them. This is because people have different views about what behaviours/activities constitute abuse. Workers may come across a situation where they think a client is a victim of abuse but another person may believe that the actions are perfectly acceptable.

Therefore, at the beginning of any training session it is good to start with some exercises which make people consider what the word 'abuse' means to them. Over the years typical responses to me as a trainer at the end of a session have been:

> *I never realized there were so many types of abuse*
>
> *I've suddenly realized I've been abusing people*

I always say that every human being is abused in some way at some point in their life. This often meets with mixed reactions. One course participant was quite offended when I said this and was adamant that she had *never* been abused. By the end of the workshop she said to me 'You were right. I have been abused'. Abuse is often not seen as abuse because it is thought to be the norm. We all accept situations and things which happen to us, which other people think are unacceptable. We must think of examples ourselves in order to understand why victims of abuse may think their situation is normal. Much abuse is subtle and may be considered 'minor'. The fact is that it is still abuse.

Workers need to learn to think more broadly; otherwise, they might miss cases of abuse and continue to think that some situations are 'normal' or 'acceptable'. Exercise 1.1 will help workers to start thinking how they have been abused or are currently being abused.

Table 1.1 shows some typical responses to Exercise 1.1 taken from various training sessions

DEFINITIONS

Once workers have considered abuse to themselves they need to be led on to think about definitions and categories of abuse. For a very long time, Mervyn Eastman was the pioneer in highlighting that old age abuse (as it was termed then) was an

---

Table 1.1 Some ways in which workers think they have been abused

- I have to make the breakfast every morning. No-one ever brings me a cup of tea in bed

- Being taken for granted

- Being taken advantage of

- Having no choice

- I cook. Nobody washes up

- Having to go shopping on my own when there is a car sitting at home

- Having to do everything yourself

- Being a taxi for everyone

- I've got an idle 22-year-old son who never tidies up

- I can never get to the TV's remote control and they hide it from me when they go out so I cannot use it

- Being disrespectful

- Manipulation

- By politicians; by advertising; by colleagues; by people we work for

- Knowing that I'll always say 'yes' to cover other people's shifts

- Never telling me I'm doing a good job

- If people criticize it knocks your confidence

- Being ignored

- Not being listened to

---

important issue in the United Kingdom (Eastman 1984). In the 1980s it was generally thought that there were three categories of abuse – **physical**, **emotional** and **financial**. Eastman defined old age abuse as:

> The systematic maltreatment, physical, emotional or financial, of an elderly person…this may take the form of physical assault, threatening behaviour, neglect, abandonment or sexual assault. (p.3)

However, as more research has been carried out and people in general have become more aware that elder abuse is a broader and more complex issue than originally thought, it is now accepted that there are two more important categories – **neglect** and **sexual** (see Handouts 1.1 and 1.2). Historically, these types of abuse were put in the category of physical abuse. It is important to give recognition to these two forms of abuse, but people sometimes find it confusing to categorize abuse because there is often overlap between categories; for example, ignoring someone is emotional abuse but it also neglect; depriving someone of medication is physical abuse but it is also neglect.

The 1990s saw the turning point in working with elder abuse in this country. In 1991 the Association of Directors of Social Services produced the *Adults at Risk* guidelines (ADSS 1991) and two years later the Social Services Inspectorate (1993) published national guidelines which described abuse:

> …as physical, sexual, psychological or financial. It may be intentional or unintentional, or the result of neglect. It causes harm to the older person, either temporarily or over a period of time. (p.3)

The crucial words in this definition are **unintentional** and **temporary**. There are many people who may be considered to be abusers because of their behaviour towards someone, but they may be acting in this way for a number of reasons; for example, lack of explanation, advice, education, training and so on. That is to say it is not their fault that they are abusing someone; it is 'unintentional'.

CASE EXAMPLES

A daughter roughly handles her demented mother. This results in bruising on her arms. The daughter was never shown how to lift her mother correctly after she suffered a stroke.

Malcolm leaves his wife, Martha, sitting in a chair in the conservatory all day. He never encourages her to walk. No one has explained that if Martha was encouraged to walk with a zimmer frame, her mobility might improve.

A sixteen-year-old care assistant has started working in a nursing home. She has no training and is told to watch how 'the others do it'. She does not dress the doubly incontinent residents from the waist downwards and leaves residents sitting on the toilet for fifteen minutes at a time.

The word **temporary** in the definition can refer to one-off incidents. This gives importance to actions which may result from stress. In the past many such incidents may have been ignored or swept under the carpet. They now have to be taken seriously, without frightening people to death. Unfortunately, the media often portray social workers in a bad light. A carer commenting on a draft document of elder abuse guidelines produced by the local social services department asked 'Won't social workers be dragging carers off to the local police station?'. No, they will not, but carers under stress need to be given proper assessment in order to provide them with resources and prevent abusive situations. All incidents have to be taken seriously. We can never be a hundred per cent sure that it is never going to happen again. Consequently, this new definition moved us on from Eastman's original definition which talked about 'systematic maltreatment'.

THE CATEGORIES OF ABUSE

Physical Abuse

Physical abuse is usually inflicted by the hands, feet or an implement, which will result in an injury or injuries to the body. Where abuse is premeditated and deliberate the injuries are usually inflicted on the trunk of the body which is very well hidden. This is why identification by home care staff and residential staff is very common because they do have access to an older person's body when they wash, bath, dress/undress them. Other professionals, like a social worker, do not see an older person's body very often and therefore do not have the opportunity to identify injuries. But there are also other forms of physical abuse, which are listed in Handout 1.3

In order to identify this type of abuse it is imperative that all staff keep concise records, which monitor situations when they suspect abuse. This will be discussed further in Chapters 3 and 5.

Emotional Abuse

Emotional abuse is very easy to achieve when an older person is made vulnerable, because of being heavily dependent or physically/mentally incapacitated. Very often the abuser has some sort of power over the older person and therefore can carry out emotional abuse in many subtle ways. The older person will often accept what is happening to them because they feel they cannot change anything and that it is their 'lot in life'. I think that historically professionals have not been very good at offering older people choices and spending time with them to work on these areas. Consequently, many older people choose to stay in the abusive situation.

CASE EXAMPLE

Betty was a very private person and had never liked going out to socialize. She considered herself a 'a real homebird'. The only person who visited her was her grandson, Ian, who came every Thursday at 12.00 to eat the sandwich Betty made for him. He then cashed her pension and said he paid all the bills. In fact, Ian was financially abusing his grandmother, but Betty would not do anything about it because she lived for 12.00 every Thursday when she would see Ian.

Even if a worker and a victim want to do something about emotional abuse through the criminal justice system, it is hard to prove, especially in a court of law. Handout 1.4 lists forms of emotional abuse and a useful exercise is to ask workers how would they prove these things happened to someone with whom they were working.

Financial Abuse

Financial abuse is probably one of the most common forms of elder abuse. This is because it is so easy to 'con' an older person, especially someone who is housebound and has to be dependent on other people to handle their financial affairs.

Financial abuse can take many forms (see Handout 1.5). It is important to remember that it is not only people out there in the community who abuse in this way, it can also be professionals. Older people are seen as 'easy targets', because they are often housebound, confused, physically or mentally disabled. It is easy to tell an older person who has not been out of the house for five years that a loaf of bread costs one pound; how will that older person know that you can buy a loaf of bread for 45p in a large supermarket?

Financial abuse can occur with small amounts of money (for example saying the shopping cost £10 when it only cost £5) or for substantial amounts of money (for example persuading someone to put their bank account into joint names and then withdrawing vast sums of money).

It is a very worrying fact that complete strangers can and do befriend isolated older people:

CASE EXAMPLE

Eddie was a middle aged painter/decorator, who could charm all the older women he worked for. He always assured them that he specialized in working for 'pensioners' and gave them 'special rates'. The women loved him because he made a real fuss of them and offered to collect their pension and do some shopping for them. He always visited them after he had finished the job. He then persuaded them that he could continue helping them by cashing their pensions and putting any savings in the bank or post office. What he did not tell them was that he was putting the money into **his** bank account.

Neglect

Historically, **neglect** was put under physical abuse, but it is now recognized that neglect can be **physical** or **emotional** (see examples given above and Handout 1.6). It has always been difficult to prove neglect in child abuse cases and the same is true of elder abuse cases. Often people do not take neglect very seriously:

Oh she's only neglected a little bit. Does it really matter?

He's been like that for years, so what?

She used to it. It's her way of life now.

Again, neglect is a form of abuse which must be dealt with by careful monitoring. Workers must never walk away from situations because they assume that nothing can be done.

Sexual Abuse

Sexual abuse is still very much a taboo subject and it is extremely hard to identify. Workers often find it difficult to imagine that a human being would sexually abuse an older person and find it even more difficult to think about the actual acts that may have occurred. It is useful for workers to have a definition of sexual abuse, which is given in Handout 1.7

A useful exercise which can be done when participants feel a bit more comfortable with each other is Exercise 1.2. This exercise makes participants think about what could happen to someone who is sexually abused.

It is important for workers to be aware of definitions and the categories of abuse, but they need to be moved on to think about situations they may come across in the course of their work. Exercise 1.3 is designed to achieve this.

Suggested Reading

Pritchard, J. (1995) 'What is abuse?' In *The Abuse of Older People*, 2nd edition. London: Jessica Kingsley. Chapter 1.

Biggs, S., Phillipson, C. and Kingston, P. (1995) 'Definitions and risk factors.' In *Elder Abuse in Perspective*. Buckingham: Open University Press. Chapter 3.

Association of Directors of Social Services (1991) *Adults at Risk*. Lancaster: ADSS.

Eastman, M. (1984) *Old Age Abuse*. London: Age Concern.

Glendenning, F. (1993) 'What is elder abuse and neglect?' In P. Decalmer and F. Glendenning (eds) *The Mistreatment of Elderly People*. London: Sage.

Social Services Inspectorate (1993) *No Longer Afraid: The Safeguard of Older People in Domestic Settings*. London: HMSO.

Participants should be provided with local guidelines/policies on working with elder abuse if they are available. Otherwise good examples are provided in Appendix of Pritchard, J. (1995) *The Abuse of Older People*, 2nd edition. London: Jessica Kingsley.

Definitions

The systematic maltreatment, physical, emotional or financial, of an elderly person...this may take the form of physical assault, threatening behaviour, neglect, abandonment or sexual assault.

> (FROM: Eastman, M. (1984) *Old Age Abuse.* London: Age Concern, p.3)

Abuse may be described as physical, sexual, psychological or financial. It may be intentional or unintentional, or the result of neglect. It causes harm to the older person, either temporarily or over a period of time.

> (FROM: Social Services Inspectorate, Department of Health (1993) *No Longer Afraid: The Safeguard of Older People in Domestic Settings.* London: HMSO, p.3)

Five Categories of Elder Abuse

PHYSICAL

EMOTIONAL

FINANCIAL

NEGLECT

SEXUAL

Physical Abuse

Injuries   bruises, cuts, lacerations, fractures, slap marks, kick marks, black eyes, burns

Assaults   physical assaults which do not result in actual injuries; force feeding

Medication (i) over medicating causing excessive drowsiness/sleep

or

(ii) not giving someone enough medication so it causes a crisis and possibly a forced admission to hospital

Malnutrition/dehydration

not feeding someone appropriately, causing weight loss

Emotional Abuse

- Humiliation

- Intimidation

- Ridicule

- Causing fear/mental anguish/anxiety

- Threats/threatening behaviour

- Bullying

- Verbal abuse e.g. shouting, swearing

- Harassment

- Lack of acknowledgment

- Isolation/withholding social contact

- Denial of basic rights e.g. choice, opinion, privacy

- Being over protected – not allowed to do things, kept back

Financial Abuse

- Cash is stolen

- Pension book is taken

- Benefit/pension is cashed and all/or part of the money is not given to the older person

- A person says that something cost more than it did (e.g. the shopping)

- A person is made appointee (through the Department of Social Security) or acquires power of attorney (through the Court of Protection) and then withholds money from the older person

- Money is withheld to such a degree that the older person does not have enough money to buy food, pay bills, rent etc

- A person says they are doing the shopping, paying bills, rent etc, but they are not

- A person is persuaded/forced to transfer money, bank/building society accounts, property, assets, financial affairs over to another person

- An older person is not allowed to be admitted to residential care by a relative who is expecting to inherit money/property when the older person dies.

Neglect

- Lack of basic care

- Not dressing someone (e.g. from the waist down because they are doubly incontinent)

- Not dressing someone appropriately (e.g. wearing thin clothes in winter)

- Refusing to buy new clothes for someone who has gained/lost weight

- Lack of food/drink

- Being left to sit in urine/faeces

- Absence of mobility aids (e.g. stick, zimmer frame) so the person's movements are restricted

- Isolation e.g. person may be locked in a room or confined space with only basic necessities (commode, bed) but no luxuries (carpet, radio, television. books, magazines)

- No social contact, stimulation.

Definition of Sexual Abuse

Sexual abuse occurs when an older person is involved in sexual activities to which they have not consented or, if they are in a confused state, do not truly comprehend.

Sexual Abuse

- Inappropriate touching

- Fondling

- Kissing

- Oral contact

- Genital contact

- Digital penetration (vagina or anus)

- Rape (vagina or anus)

- Penetration with objects

- Exploitation

- Pornography – forced to participate in; forced to watch videos, read magazines etc.

- Ritual/satanic abuse

HOW HAVE I BEEN ABUSED?

Objective

To make participants think how they have been abused in very subtle ways either at home or at work.

Participants

Exercise to be carried out in a large group

Equipment

Flipchart paper and pens

Time

20 minutes for brainstorming and full discussion

Task

Participants are asked to give examples of how they have been abused.

Instructions for Trainer

This exercise can raise some very sensitive issues. The trainer should never force participants to contribute to this exercise and also s/he should make it safe for anyone to take time out from the group. The trainer should also ensure that all participants feel OK at the end of the exercise.

WHAT IS SEXUAL ABUSE?

Objective

To make participants think about the acts which could be involved in sexual abuse, that is, what could actually happen to a victim of sexual abuse. The purpose of the exercise is to prepare participants for what they could encounter in the future if one of their clients is sexually abused.

Participants

To work on their own initially

Equipment

Paper and pens

Time

5 minutes to make personal lists

5 minutes to share list with a partner

5 minutes to share lists and discuss Handout 1.8

Task

Participants are asked to make a list of what they think sexual abuse is. They must focus on the acts/activities rather than emotional terminology.

NOTE FOR TRAINERS: many participants feel very uncomfortable doing this exercise. It must be emphasized to participants that it is not a test and even if they only write down one thing on the list then that is OK. The trainer should also check that everyone feels OK at the end of the exercise.

ABUSE OR NOT ABUSE?

Objective

To make participants think about what constitutes abuse

Participants

Exercise to be carried out in small groups

Equipment

Prepare photocopies of handout with situations to be considered

Time

Groups spend 3 minutes on each situation (30 minutes in total).

The trainer takes feedback by going through each scenario and finding out what each group's consensus was and was there any disagreement in the group.

Task

Each group will consider and discuss the scenarios on the hand-out. It is the task of the group to reach a consensus of opinion about whether this is a case of abuse or not. If the group agrees it is abuse, they must decide which category (or categories) of abuse i.e. physical, emotional, financial, neglect, sexual, the case fits in to.

Abuse or not Abuse?

1.   Everyday Samuel, who is Jewish and was imprisoned in a German concentration camp during the Second World War, is visited by his 16-year-old grandson. The grandson likes to sneak up behind his grandfather and shout 'The Germans are coming'.

2.   A daughter says to her mother 'If you don't stop messing the bed I'll get you put away in one of those old people's homes'.

3.   Mr Eyres arranges for his mother's private works pension to be paid into his own bank account and says he is saving for her funeral. Mrs Eyres would like to spend a week by the seaside, but her son says she cannot afford it.

4.   A neighbour regularly shops for the old people living on the same landing in a high rise block of flats. She takes two pounds for herself out of the money she is given for shopping but does not tell the old people she is doing this.

5.   A district nurse and a carer talk about Edith and her condition in front of Edith, but do not include her in the conversation.

6.   Rosemary is very weak and unsteady on her feet, but she would love to try to walk around her garden with a zimmer frame to look at the flowers. Her daughter says she must remain in the house.

7.   A daughter says her father only needs two hot meals a week.

8.   Percy is obsessed with his bowels and is always wanting to go to the toilet. His wife has got very fed up, so every time she takes him to the toilet she leaves him there for 30 minutes.

9.   Philip masturbates in front of his 74-year-old mother every day; he does not have sexual intercourse with her.

10. Mrs Anders gets very agitated the week before she is due to go in for a respite stay. Her husband gives her extra medication to calm her down, but she does not realize this.

© Jacki Pritchard, 1996

2 Recognizing Abuse

It is not easy to identify elder abuse, because it is often inflicted subtlety by the abuser. This is especially true if the abuse is premeditated. Abuse can happen for any number of reasons and it is important that a worker has an understanding of possible causal factors of abuse in order to work with a case of elder abuse. I always say that working with elder abuse is like doing a 5000 piece jigsaw; it takes ages to put it together and at the end there may be a piece missing so you never get the full picture. Likewise when working with a case of elder abuse – you can suspect abuse is going on but cannot be sure; and this situation can go on for years. This is why it is crucial that where there is a suspicion that abuse is occurring, the situation must be **monitored** and **reviewed** regularly.

The aim of this chapter is to help workers develop skills in recognizing abuse. Most guidelines which exist on abuse have lists of indicators and possible causes of abuse. Training needs to address these lists, but before doing so it is important that time is spent with workers explaining crucial facts like:

- **abuse can happen anywhere**

- **there are no social or class barriers**

- **it is wrong to stereotype the typical victim and typical abuser**

- **abuse can be premeditated/deliberate**

- **abuse is not just related to carers' stress**

Workers must come to realize that elder abuse can be a very complex issue. Victims are often vulnerable and are therefore easy targets, so they can be in a situation where they may suffer more than one form of abuse and in some cases there can be more than one abuser involved.

CASE EXAMPLE

✝ ✝ Louisa was highly dependent because she had suffered several strokes, the effects of which were she could not walk and her speech was limited. She also suffered from dementia. Her sister came to live with her in order to be the primary carer, but she neglected her. Louisa was kept isolated in her bedroom 24 hours a day. When an elder abuse investigation took place, it was proven that Louisa was neglected by her sister, but she was also physically abused on a regular basis by two home helps who visited her in the mornings to wash and dress her.

Although everyone wants to protect an older person who is being abused it is important not to rush in and make things worse. Assessment of the situation should be done carefully and not be hurried. It is important to gather bits if information (the pieces of the jigsaw), by looking at the past as well as the current situation. The root cause of abuse frequently relates back to something which has happened in the past. Again this is why I have to stress that home care and residential/day care staff are crucial in working with elder abuse. People talk and confide in these workers and they might have been told about a family feud/fall out or the abuser's history of problems (e.g. alcoholism, gambling, drug addiction, mental health, debts etc). Handout 2.1 is a list of key issues which workers need to keep in the forefront of their minds.

It is necessary to dispel some myths about victims and abusers that have been created over the years. It has been very trendy to stereotype victims and abusers both in child abuse work and in elder abuse work, but it is wrong to do so.

Everyone has mental pictures which they carry around in their heads. When words are said visual images are created in our minds. 'Victim' and 'abuser' are very emotive words which are used extensively during any course which is focused on the subject of abuse. Exercise 2.1 is designed to bring out workers' thoughts (and maybe myths) about victims and abusers.

After the exercise has taken place, Handout 2.2 should be given out to explain the stereotypes which have been created. Handouts 2.3 and 2.4 can then be used by the trainer to illustrate how these stereotypes are not helpful.

Workers have to be taught what signs to look for in identifying abuse and this is often difficult because abuse can be very well hidden both by the victim and the abuser. This information can be difficult to assimilate and it can be helpful for workers to have checklists, which can be used at a later date when they suspect that a client is being abused. I have designed some checklists which workers can refer back to in Handouts 2.5, 2.6 and 2.7.

Regarding physical abuse, workers are not expected to become medical experts and diagnose whether injuries are accidental or non accidental. However, in Chapter 5 I discuss the importance of recording injuries and using monitoring tools. Consequently, it is important in training sessions to have some discussion about injuries and their location on the body. Workers need to realize what awful things can happen to a victim of elder abuse. This can often be very distressing for workers participating in a training session, because they may never have dreamt of anything so awful. However, it is necessary to have some discussion or they may fail to recognize abusive situations. Therefore, they need to know certain basic facts like there are different types of bruising:

e.g.   finger tip bruising

grasp marks

outline bruising (perhaps from a stick, belt, shoe)

and burns

e.g.   cigarette burns

dunking burns (hands/feet being immersed in boiling hot water)

outline burns (hot water pipe, radiator, iron)

Useful information and materials regarding identifying injuries are available else-where (Decalmer 1993; Bennett 1994).

It is extremely difficult to identify sexual abuse. Telltale signs are often left on a person's underclothes, nightwear. If a person has frequent infections/dis-charges/bleeding a doctor should be consulted. It is very important to get the victim examined as soon as possible. Obviously with someone who is mentally sound you must have his/her permission to contact the doctor. Unfortunately, many times examinations do not take place and hasty diagnoses are often the norm – for example thrush or piles!

It must be stressed that if a confused person discloses that they have been sexually abused, it must be taken seriously. Sometimes we shall never know if the person is talking about something that is happening to them now or relating back to something that happened earlier in their life. But, *too many* cases have not been followed up because the person has not been mentally sound and then sexual abuse has been proven years later. Police surgeons are the most skilled people in this area of work, so it is often best to have police involvement so that they can obtain the police surgeon's expertise.

Financial abuse is probably one of the most difficult things to prove. It is very difficult to get evidence that:

o **somebody is taking money or assets**

o **an older person's money is being used inappropriately or not for what it is intended**

o **someone is not paying the bills as promised**

o **money is genuinely disappearing**

In this country we do not have specific legislation regarding financial abuse and older people. We have to rely on the criminal justice system and the police to gather evidence of theft, fraud, deception and so forth. This is extremely difficult if the victim is confused and cannot be asked about their financial arrangements.

Also it is very difficult to work with situations where we might feel an older person is being abused financially by a relative but they feel it is their duty to do what the relative says.

CASE EXAMPLES

✝✝ Mrs G is scared living in the community now because she is immobile and housebound and local kids keep breaking into her house. She has said on many occasions that she would like to become a permanent resident in the home where she goes for respite care. Her daughter says she 'must not' go into care because she will have to sell her house and use her savings to pay for the care and that according to the daughter is 'my inheritance'.

✝✝ Every-time John visits his grandmother, Thelma, he talks to her about his financial problems and the fact that he is finding it difficult to pay the bills and clothe his children. In the past year he has asked Thelma to lend him money to pay for two holidays, a car for his wife and for a garden shed to be built in the garden. Thelma has always given him the money because 'he deserves nice things' but she has gone without things she would like for herself.

One of the most crucial factors in identifying abuse is seeing and monitoring changes in behaviour. Of course this can only be achieved by a person who knows the victim well, because it is necessary to know what the victim was like before the changes started taking place. This is the why I keep stressing that home care and residential/day care staff are so important in identifying abuse. Some typical changes are listed in Handout 2.9.

Finally, although it has been stated above that abuse can be premeditated and deliberate we must not forget that some elder abuse is related to carer's stress. I have to emphasize, however, that people must not think that elder abuse is only related to carers' stress. In the past we have thought too narrowly about the cause of elder abuse and from what has already been said there can be many root causes of abuse both in the past and in the current situation. It is useful for workers to think about what might cause the carer stress (see Pritchard 1991). Handout 2.10 can be used as a basis for discussion.

Suggested Reading

Eastman, M. (1984) 'What is old age abuse?' In *Old Age Abuse*. London: Age Concern, Chapter 2.

Pritchard, J. (1995) 'Recognizing abuse.' In *The Abuse of Older People*, 2nd edition. London: Jessica Kingsley, Chapter 2.

Biggs, S., Phillipson, C. and Kingston, P. (1995) 'Definitions and risk factors.' In *Elder Abuse in Perspective*. Buckingham: Open University Press, Chapter 3.

References

Bennett, G. (1994) 'Clinical diagnosis and treatment.' In M. Eastman (ed) *Old Age Abuse: A New Perspective*. London: Chapman and Hall.

Decalmer, P. (1993) 'Clinical presentation.' In P. Decalmer and F. Glendenning (eds) *The Mistreatment of Elderly People*. London: Sage.

Eastman, M. (1988) 'Granny abuse.' In *Community Outlook* October, 15–16.

Gelles, R.J. and Cornell, C.P. (1985) *Intimate Violence in Families*. Beverley Hills, Ca: Sage.

Glendenning, F. (1993) 'What is elder abuse and neglect?' In P. Decalmer and F. Glendenning (eds) *The Mistreatment of Elderly People*. London: Sage.

Pritchard, J. (1991) 'Charting the hits.' *Care Weekly* 9th October, 10–11.

Social services Inspectorate (1993) *No Longer Afraid: The Safeguard of Older People in Domestic Settings*. London: HMSO.

Some Key Issues
to Think About

Do not just focus on the victim, because it maybe the abuser who has problems rather than the victim

Social histories of the victim and abuser can be helpful in looking back at the past

Has there been a history of child abuse in the family?

Has there been a history of marital violence?

Is the carer under stress and in what way(s)?

Stereotype: Victim

The majority are female, over 80 and are dependent as a result of physical or mental incapacity

(From: Eastman, M. (1984) *Old Age Abuse*. London: Age Concern, p.41)

Stereotype: Abuser

The abuser is typically identified as being female, middle aged and usually the offspring of the abused

(From: Gelles, R.J. and Cornell, C.P. (1985) *Intimate Violence in Families*. Beverley Hills, CA: Sage, p.104)

Pen Pictures – Victims

Joshua was a gay man, who had suffered a stroke and lived by himself. He liked to talk about his past life and felt frustrated because he had no family or friends. He became very vulnerable because he welcomed strangers into his house. Over the years he was financially and sexually abused by different young men, but also gangs of youths.

Mentally sound Mrs H, aged 80, was a double amputee who had always been cared for by her husband until he died suddenly. She was subsequently abused physically, emotionally and financially by her brother, who came to live with her. She was reluctant to take any action even though she had to ask permission to move from one room to another. He frequently attacked her and threatened to cut off her cat's ears.

When Mrs D was 84 years old she discovered that she had breast cancer and underwent a mastectomy. She was the sole carer for her demented husband. Mr D continued to abuse his frail wife as he had done since their wedding night 65 years ago.

Mrs T was in her sixties and lived with her three sons. She suffered from epileptic fits and had had a stroke which affected her left side. She was mentally sound, but immobile. Her sons locked her in her bedroom all day and never got her dressed.

Emilio, aged 73 years, was well known in the local community and described as a 'wino' and 'a waste of space'. Little help had been given to him by professionals. He was financially abused by a neighbour who had befriended him. After a formal elder abuse investigation had taken place, the assessment indicated that Emilio was not an alcoholic but was suffering from a mental health problem.

Ida had always had a good relationship with her grandson, who had lived with her since his mother got divorced. However, once Ida had had a stroke and could not get out and about with her grandson, he started to physically abuse her 'because she wasn't fun anymore'.

Pen Pictures – Abusers

19-year-old Kevin physically and financially abused his 77-year-old grandmother. He hit her, but also neglected her in that he ate all the food in the house, so she was often left starving. He cashed her pension so she never had any money for herself.

Julie was a 22-year-old day centre worker, who was well liked by all the users because of her lively personality and sense of humour. She was always willing to do additional work, for example, extra shifts as escort on the minibus and home visits to users when they were sick and had not attended day centre. What came to light eventually was that Julie was stealing from clients when she went to visit them in their homes.

Harold was in his fifties and had always had a sexual relationship with his mother. He did not like it when his mother became confused and refused to have him in her bed anymore, so he raped her.

11-year-old Jonathan liked to act older than his age and hung around with boys older than himself. He and three other youths knew an older man in the community who was said to be 'simple'. The four boys used to break into the old man's house at night, tie him to the table, hit him, burn him with cigarettes and urinate over him.

Len was a social worker in his mid thirties, who was married with three children. He had taken on too many commitments including a large mortgage, HP agreements etc. He started taking agency work in addition to his full-time job, but still could not pay his debts. He subsequently financially abused his confused older clients and also adults with learning disabilities over a period of three years.

Mr W appeared to be a very successful businessman when he bought a new house and car. He visited his mother regularly, cashed her pension and said that he paid all her bills. Mrs W then received letters threatening gas and electricity disconnections. Mr W was eventually charged with defrauding the Department of Social Security and the Inland Revenue.

© Jacki Pritchard, 1996

Physical Indications of Abuse

(this includes physical neglect)

- Multiple bruising, not consistent with a fall

- Black eyes, slap marks, kick marks, other bruises

- Burns, not consistent with scorching by direct heat

- Fractures not consistent with falls

- Stench of urine or faeces

- Indications of malnutrition or over-feeding

- Absence of mobility aids

- Administration of inappropriate drugs or the absence of necessary medication

© Jacki Pritchard, 1996

Indicators of Sexual Abuse

- Genital or urinary irritation

- Frequent infections (evidence of vaginal discharge may be found on knickers)

- Bleeding (blood can be found on underwear, nightclothes)

- Sexually transmitted disease

- Bruising on inner thighs

- Difficulty in walking/sitting

- Sudden onset of confusion

- Depression

- Nightmares

- Severe upset or agitation when the older person is being bathed, dressed, undressed, or medically examined (or when these things are suggested)

- Conversation regularly becomes of a sexual nature

Indicators
of Emotional Abuse

(this includes emotional neglect)

- Insomnia/deprivation of sleep or need for excessive sleep

- Change in appetite

- Unusual weight gain/loss

- Weepiness/unusual bouts of sobbing/crying

- Unexplained paranoia

- Low self-esteem

- Excessive fear/anxiety

- Ambivalence

Indicators
of Financial Abuse

- Unexplained or sudden inability to pay bills (e.g. rent, gas, electricity, no money for food/shopping)

- Unexplained or sudden withdrawal of money from post office/bank/building society accounts

- Disparity between assets and satisfactory living conditions

- Lack of receptivity by the older person or relative/neighbour to any necessary assistance requiring expenditure, when finances are not a problem

- Extraordinary interest by family members and other people in the older person's assets/will

Known Reactions to Abuse

- The denial (often forthright) that anything is amiss, with an accompanying emphasis that things 'have never been better'.

- Resignation, stoicism, and, sometimes, an acceptance of incidents as being part of being old/vulnerable

- Withdrawal from activity, communication and participation

- Marked change in behaviour and inappropriate attachments. Fear, subsequently combined with depression and a sense of hopelessness

- Mental confusion

- Anger and physical/verbal outbursts

- Seeking (attention/protection), often from numerous sources (some of which can be unlikely)

Carer's Stress

WHAT PUSHES THEM OVER THE EDGE?

- Behaviour traits of the older person

- The nature of the tasks that have to be performed on a daily basis

- Frustration experienced by the carer

- The carer's sense of isolation

- Lack of services and/or other community support

(For further discussion see Jacki Pritchard 'Charting the hits', *Care Weekly,* 9th October 1991, pp.10–11)

ROGUES GALLERY

Objective

To encourage participants to be honest about who they think may be a victim of elder abuse and who might actually abuse an older person

Participants

Exercise to be carried in small groups. Ideally 4–5 in a group. Four groups if possible.

Equipment

Paper and pencils

Large flipchart paper and coloured pens

Sellotape, blutack

Time

Groups spend 15 minutes carrying out the task.

Participants spend 5 minutes looking at each other's portraits.

Followed by discussion of images created.

Task

Two groups are asked to think about a 'typical victim'; the other two groups are to think about a 'typical abuser'. Participants have to write down on a flipchart sheet words which describe the characteristics and physical appearance of the victim or abuser. When they have exhausted their list of words, they have to draw a portrait of their victim/abuser. The portraits are then displayed on the walls.

3 What to do when Working with Elder Abuse

Everybody dreads coming across a case of abuse, especially after they have done a training course and they are aware that abuse can happen anywhere. Therefore, every worker needs to be prepared and to feel confident that s/he knows what to do and when. If procedures exist within a department it is important that all home care staff and residential/day care workers know of their existence and are familiar with them. They need to know what could happen when and if an elder abuse investigation takes place. It is therefore crucial that training is provided on procedures and this needs to be done in an imaginative way so that workers are not made to feel it is 'boring'. They must remember what to do! This chapter gives a general framework for investigating elder abuse. The following chapter goes into more detail about practice skills.

Residential and home care staff may have a supportive role to play. For example, if a victim discloses to them and they do want some intervention, the person who heard the initial disclosure may be the person who has to keep explaining what might happen in the future. Handout 3.1 is an outline of what may happen if an elder abuse investigation does take place. Obviously there may be variations within departments but this is a typical structure which could be given as a simple example for staff.

REFERRING ON

It is crucial that workers are told and constantly reminded that if they have any concerns/anxieties they should talk to their manager. It is not helpful to anyone to keep things bottled up. Most of us work on gut reactions initially and even if a worker has not got concrete evidence that abuse is taking place they should vent their feelings about this.

It is also very important to write down facts even at a very early stage. Workers should log anything they are concerned about, for example:

(1) If Mrs X seems to be getting a lot of bruises, a worker should keep a record of when the bruising was seen, what it was like and where it was located on the body (see Chapter 5 for more discussion on use of bodycharts).

(2) Even if a worker notices slight changes in a client's behaviour these should be noted down – for example, a client becomes very weepy or maybe withdrawn or alternatively physically aggressive.

Many workers feel uncomfortable about doing this because they feel they are breaking confidentiality. They have to be honest with their client. If they have concerns they should have tried to discuss them with the client in the first place. Workers should also be honest about the records they keep.

If a client starts to disclose about abuse the worker must immediately remind them about the boundaries of confidentiality – in other words that the worker has to inform his/her line manager. Workers should always have explained these boundaries at the beginning of their involvement with the client. I am sure this does not always happen and it can make life difficult later on when a disclosure is heard. The client who has started to disclose will either continue or shut up completely. The latter reaction is unfortunate but it does give the worker scope to do some follow up work in the future. A victim will only disclose to someone they trust and building trust can take time. I believe that sometimes it can take four to five years for some victims to disclose.

When a worker has talked to his/her manager, s/he may suggest the situation is monitored carefully in the future if there is insufficient evidence to investigate, or if there is cause for concern the manager may wish to refer the matter on to the social services area office. If the client is mentally sound all this should be discussed with the client in the first instance as they may not want any intervention. It may be necessary for the worker, who has heard the initial disclosure or who has suspicions, to go and talk to the client again. Workers have to be honest about what processes may follow. The worker who has initially set off the process needs to know what may happen next for his/her sake as well as the client's.

A social worker should *never* go rushing out to interview the victim before gathering some information. Neither should s/he share information about the alleged abuse at this stage because it may be totally unfounded. Workers have constantly to remind themselves that **elder abuse is not the same as child abuse**. We have no statutory rights and we cannot share information in the same way. We are dealing with *adults* not children. At the gathering information stage no one has talked to the alleged victim. It is always useful to remind workers that none of us would like it if a group of professionals started talking about us behind our backs and discussing the possibility that we might be a victim of abuse.

It is the social work manager's task to decide how to proceed. In Handout 3.1 I have stated that decisions must be made about strategy, for example about who will visit and whether the police will be involved at this early stage. The police are not usually involved at this early stage because the victim has not been interviewed formally and may not wish for the police's involvement. However, if it is a very serious case where the client (and workers) are at serious risk of violence the police would be brought in to go out on the initial visit. I have to say that I have trained many police personnel and they have said they would prefer to be contacted earlier on rather than after social workers have done several interviews.

It is advisable for two people to visit for a number of reasons. First, the safety of workers has to be of paramount importance – very often they do not know what they are walking into and no worker should be put at risk. Second, both the victim and abuser may be present, so in some situations one worker can focus on the victim and the other on the abuser because various emotions could be present, for example anger, upset, bewilderment. It is easier to have two people to calm the situation down. Third, sometimes workers need to refer back to base to get advice from a manager or to seek a place of safety. If a telephone is not available in the victim's house, then one of the workers will need to find the nearest public phone box. Good practice would indicate that once an interview has taken place the victim (who could be extremely distressed at this stage) should not be left alone until s/he knows what is going to happen next. Fourth, it is helpful to have two workers present because it helps in the assessment and the analysis of the interview(s).

There is the counter argument that two people going in is 'too heavy', 'gestapo like', 'intimidating for the client'. This can be true if a social worker is involved already and then suddenly turns up with someone else. Also, it can be daunting for the client if two complete strangers land on the doorstep. However, it need not be a horrendous experience if workers have specialist training on how to interview abuse victims in an appropriate manner.

But who should visit? Who are the two people? Most departments now say there should be one qualified social worker plus one other person. If the police are going to be involved early on a police officer will be the other person. If the alleged victim does not have a social worker, the other person should be someone that they know/feel comfortable with, for example GP, district nurse, home care organizer, day centre worker or the person who heard the initial disclosure (this could be the home care assistant, a residential care assistant).

It is important that from the outset that the two workers are honest and upfront with the victim about *why* they are there. It is useful to interview the victim alone (i.e., not with the alleged abuser present) but good practice would ensure that the victim is asked if they would like anyone in particular present during the interview, for example a friend, neighbour or advocate. The issue of confidentiality should also be discussed with the victim at this stage. At the end of each interview the victim should be told what will happen next, that is, what the workers are going to do after they leave, if they will visit again and if so when, possibility of a case conference and so on (without frightening the victim to death!).

Some victims may become confused at this stage. They may forget what they have been told and will not remember what may happen next. They might also change their mind about future involvement, making a statement to the police and so on. It is here that home care and residential staff may have a supportive role to play. They may need to explain again what might happen in the future or they just might have to be there to listen and support the victim in his/her decision.

Victims may have to be interviewed several times and it is important that throughout this process they are reminded about what will happen next and what could happen in the future. A worker should never leave them not knowing when they will be contacted again. Again, this is when home care and residential have a vital supportive role to play and, therefore, they must be trained on procedures so that they know what will happen.

INVESTIGATIONS IN INSTITUTIONS

There is still a lot of debate about how investigations should be carried out in institutions. Some guidelines address this issue, others do not. Trainers/managers need to be very clear about what *should* take place in their department. Guidance is needed about:

(1) **who will carry out investigations**
at the moment there are several possibilities:

- victim's allocated social worker
- independent social worker, who has nothing to do with the home
- someone from the residential sector within the department
- officer from the inspection unit

(2) **when/how/by whom will the victim be interviewed**
sometimes two investigations might be going on – the elder abuse investigation and the disciplinary investigation (if the alleged abuser is a member of staff) – the victim must not be harassed or put under undue pressure by being interviewed several times by different personnel.

(3) **what happens when the alleged abuser is a member of staff**
re suspension, support for that member of staff etc.

THE LAW (OR LACK OF IT!)

Home care, residential and day care staff do not want to be bombarded with information about the law, but they do need to have some basic facts. There is very little legislation that is directly helpful to working with elder abuse. In this country specific legislation has not been developed. Therefore, we have to rely on the criminal justice system. Workers find this very frustrating because they naturally want to protect a client from abuse but if the client is mentally sound and does not want any help nothing can be done. It has to be emphasized time and time again that elder abuse is not like child abuse; it is not statutory work.

I have already stated that the police are often not brought in during the early stages of an investigation. If a victim does want the police involved then they need to know what might happen and what they might have to do. This is the information workers need to have and be able to pass on to a victim.

A victim needs to know that the police will want to interview him/her and s/he will need to make a written statement. Workers and clients need to know that even if the police think they have got enough evidence to proceed, when the evidence is passed to the Crown Prosecution Service (CPS) it might be thrown out. The CPS might not let the case proceed to court because 'it is not in the public's interest to do so', meaning there might not be enough good evidence/reliable witnesses. So the victim could go through a lot of trauma being interviewed, having to repeat their story many times and in the end nothing is achieved.

The victim also has to be warned that if the case does proceed to court, then s/he might have to stand up in the witness box and give evidence. This fact can dissuade victims from wanting to take things further. The other main reason why victims do not want any action taken is because they are scared that the abuser may get sent to prison. This is a daunting thought if the abuser is a relative.

Where guidelines exist, relevant legislation is usually listed. These lists can be used as a basis for discussion in a training session. There are other sources of material elsewhere (Pritchard 1995, p.60–64; Griffiths *et al.* 1993; Law Commission 1991, 1993a, 1993b, 1993c and 1996).

GOOD PRACTICE

As well as talking about the procedures and what staff are expected to do, there must be some discussion about what constitutes good practice. Many staff get on with their jobs and probably do not spend enough time (if they spend any) thinking about how they should practice, especially when working with abusive situations. Handout 3.2 can be used as a basis for discussion.

INFORMATION/LEAFLETS FOR STAFF

All this guidance is very difficult for workers to take in in one session, so it is useful to give them something to take away which will help them remember key points about working with abuse. Some authorities have produced leaflets for their staff to keep handy (such as in the pocket of their overall!). The leaflet which was designed for Wakefield Social Services homes care staff, who are known as community carers, is shown in Figure 3.1.

When managers fail to act

I hear from a number of workers (both in the home care service and residential settings) that even when they report abuse their managers do not follow it up. My advice is that if a manager does fail to act on a report, then the worker should report to a manager at a higher level. I always suggest that the worker should keep a written record of the date and time when they have reported their concerns to the first line manager, but also a factual account of what has been said. If a worker has to go to a higher level then it must be done verbally but also in a written report, so that it *has* to be dealt with. Workers feel very uncomfortable about doing this, but bad managers have to be reported otherwise tragedies will occur.

It is hard to make training on procedures exciting, but it is necessary to test out whether the information has sunk in. I have found the best way of doing this is to ask participants to do some practical exercises. Exercise 3.1 is designed to make participants think what they would actually *do* if they found themselves in a certain situation.

I have always found that doing case studies helps workers to focus on what should happen. During discussions they will highlight things they are not sure about or things they just do not know. The following case studies can be used to check whether participants are clear about procedures and what their own roles should be in certain situations.

SUGGESTED READING

Pritchard, J. (1995) 'Working with abuse.' In *The Abuse of Older People*, 2nd edition. London: Jessica Kingsley, Chapter 3.

Local guidelines should be used; if these are not available good examples of guidelines are given in Appendices 1 and 2 in Pritchard (1995).

REFERENCES

Griffiths A., Roberts G. and Williams, J. (1993) 'Elder abuse and the law.' In P. Declamer and F. Glendenning (eds) *The Mistreatment of Elderly People*. London: Sage, Chapter 3.

Law Commission (1991) *Mentally Incapacitated Adults and Decision Making: An Overview*. Consultation paper No 119. London: HMSO.

Law Commission (1993a) *Mentally Incapacitated Adults and Decision-making: A New Jurisdiction*. Consultation paper 128. London: HMSO.

Law Commission (1993b) *Mentally Incapacitated Adults and Decision-making: Medical Treatment and Research*. Consultation paper 129. London: HMSO.

Law Commission (1993c) *Mentally Incapacitated and Other Vulnerable Adults. Public Law Protection*. Consultation paper 130. London: HMSO.

Law Commission (1996) *Mental Incapacity*. Consultation paper 231. London: HMSO.

WHAT IS ELDER ABUSE

There are 5 categories of abuse:-

* PHYSICAL
* EMOTIONAL
* FINANCIAL
* SEXUAL
* NEGLECT

WHAT TO LOOK FOR

*	Bruises	*	Drowsiness
*	Fractures	*	Lack of medication
*	Slap/kick marks	*	Hunger/dehydration
*	Black eyes	*	Money problems
*	Burns	*	Denial of rights
*	Cuts/lacerations	*	Isolation
*	Weight/loss		

City of Wakefield Metropolitan District Council

ELDER ABUSE

CAN HAPPEN ANYWHERE

A simple guide
for
Community Carers

Think about how your client is?

Ask yourself:-

*   Has there been a change in behaviour/personality?

*   Are there signs of withdrawal, depression, confusion?

*   Is s/he asking for help from a lot of people?

*   What else is happening regularly
    eg visits to casualty, ringing the GP,
    admissions to hospital, injuries?

WHAT TO DO

YOU CANNOT IGNORE ABUSE

TELL YOUR RESOURCE MANAGER

GOOD PRACTICE

THINGS TO REMEMBER

*   You are bound by confidentiality

*   You are dealing with adults not children

*   Old people have basic rights i.e. choice, opinion, privacy

*   You must listen

*   Do not jump to conclusions

*   Do not be judgemental

*   Do not make accusations

*   Observe what is happening to your client

*   Never panic

*   Do not keep concerns/worries to yourself

*   Talk to your Resource Manager

Reproduced by permission of Wakefield Community and Social Services Department

Good Practice for Working with Elder Abuse

Allegation/Suspicion of Abuse:

Report to line manager, who may proceed with a

↓

Referral to the Social Services Area Office:

If case is known – goes to allocated social worker

If alleged victim not known/closed case – goes to duty social worker

Stage 1

Gathering information:

- basic facts about alleged victim/abuser

- details of incident/allegations of abuse

- who is already involved (professionals, volunteers)

(REMEMBER the boundaries of confidentiality at this stage)

Stage 2

Discussion between social worker and manager

Decision about how to proceed:

- strategy

- who will visit (2 people?)

- police involvement

- special needs e.g. interpreter, someone to sign, advocate

Stage 3

Visit to alleged victim (interview alone if possible i.e. without abuser being present) – purpose to establish facts and to assess degree of risk

Medical examination if necessary and only with the victim's consent

Further visits may be necessary

Possible interview with abuser

Stage 4

Case conference

Protection plan

Stage 5

Implementing protection plan

Monitoring

Reviewing

Good Practice

Things to Remember

- You are bound by confidentiality

- You are dealing with adults not children

- Adults have basic rights – e.g. choice, opinion, privacy

- You must listen

- Do not jump to conclusions

- Do not be judgemental

- Do not make accusations

- Observe what is happening to your client

- Never panic/keep calm

- Do not show shock or horror

- Do not keep concerns/worries to yourself

- Talk to your manager

WHAT WOULD YOU DO IF...?

Objective

To make participants think about how they would react if they found themselves in a certain situation.

Participants

Exercise to be carried out in small groups

Equipment

Handouts to be photocopied beforehand

Flipchart paper and pens

Time

30 minutes to complete the exercise

Task

Participants are asked to consider and discuss in their groups each scenario in turn and write down what they would do if they found themselves in that situation.

Some examples are given below in the handout. Some of these situations could occur either in the community or in a residential setting.

Exercise
What Would You Do If…?

1. When you walk into the lounge you see your client's husband hit her across the face.

2. When you call in at tea-time, you find Mr Ellis with a black eye, which he did not have earlier in the day.

3. As you are bathing Mrs Bennett you notice bruising on her inner thighs.

4. One of your clients who is normally very happy and talkative, has been crying a lot lately.

5. Winnie loves having her hair washed and set every week. As you are doing this today for her you notice dark line marks round her neck and also small bruises behind her ear.

6. You have taken on a new client who lives with his sister, but each time you visit he is either drowsy or asleep.

7. You hear a relative shout at a client 'I hate you because of what you did to me'.

8. Your manager will not follow up your report that Mrs Davis is being physically neglected. S/he says you are exaggerating.

9. This morning you are helping Ada to get dressed when you see blood on her nightie and running down her leg.

10. By mistake you pick up the wrong letter which a client has asked you to read. The letter is from the Housing Department stating that your client has one thousand pound rent arrears.

Case Study I

Sarah lives with her husband, Albert, in a block of high rise flats. Albert is the sole carer for Sarah, who is dementing. They receive home help one day a week for two hours. Neither Sarah nor Albert go out very much. A social worker is involved but does not visit very often.

One afternoon, a neighbour, Mrs Clarke, hears screaming and she thinks it sounds as if someone is being hit. She is frightened and unsure about what to do. A local authority old people's home is situated right opposite the block of flats, so Mrs Clarke goes there to report what she has heard.

The principal from the home, Mrs Bland, goes out immediately to Sarah and Albert's flat. When she rings the doorbell, Sarah answers the door completely in the nude. Mrs Bland is allowed in the flat and Albert says that he has reached the end of his tether. Sarah is doubly incontinent, but Albert believes 'she makes a mess deliberately'. Mrs Bland sees that Sarah has bruises on her arms and legs, and a definite hand mark in the middle of her back.

Discuss: **Was Mrs Bland right to have gone over the road?**

What else could she have done?

As she has gone, what should she do next?

What would *you* have done?

What issues need to be considered in this case?

© Jacki Pritchard, 1996

Case Study 2

You are a care assistant in an older person's home. Today a car boot sale is being held in the car park (which is located at the back of the home) in order to raise funds for the residents' summer outing.

Esther, who suffers from dementia, has been a resident in your home for the past two years. She used to live with her son, David, who is 45 years old. Esther's mental state deteriorated so much that David could no longer cope with her at home. He works full time as a sales representative and had previously been able to manage with the support from home care services.

You have been running the refreshment stall at the car boot sale, but have run out of teabags. When you go into the unit to get some fresh supplies you walk along the ground floor corridor. As you are doing this, you see Esther and David embracing but then you see David give his mother a long full kiss on the lips. You also see that David has his hands underneath his mother's blouse.

Discuss: **What do you think your initial thoughts/ reactions would be?**

What would you do next?

Make a list of actual sentences you would say to Esther and David.

Case Study 3

You are a day centre worker who sometimes goes on the mini-bus to escort users to the day centre. Today you call for Georgina, who is in her seventies and lives with her brother, Kenneth. Georgina has openly talked at the day centre about her difficulties with Kenneth. He has a drink problem and becomes very violent when he is drunk.

Georgina and Kenneth have lived together for years and Georgina, being the older sister, feels responsible for her 'little brother'. Georgina often arrives at day centre with visible bruising and on one occasion she had lacerations on her face, where Kenneth had thrown a glass at her which shattered.

When you knock on the door today Georgina shouts for you to come in. You find her lying on the lounge floor, unable to move. Apparently, Kenneth came in drunk last night and beat her very badly. He then left the house. Georgina is very distressed, but does not want to go to hospital or for you to call the doctor, because she is scared that 'they will put Kenneth away'. You believe that Georgina could have broken her leg. She does say she wants to go away somewhere safe for a while, but not to tell anyone why.

Discuss: **What would you do?**

What are the risk factors in this case?

What are the boundaries of confidentiality?

Case Study 4

You are temporary care worker and since you came to work at Walkley House you have been concerned about the behaviour and practices of two of your colleagues, Theresa and Jill. They seem to really dislike some residents and show it openly by being verbally abusive. For example they refer to the residents who are incontinent as 'the smellies' and to others as 'silly bitch', 'demented cow' and so on. Other staff tell you that this has been reported to the manager of the unit, but she has not done anything about it because she finds Theresa and Jill 'amusing'.

Yesterday, you walked into one of the bathrooms because you thought it was empty and you saw Theresa and Jill hit a resident across her back whilst she was in the bath. Immediately, you reported this to the manager who said she would speak to the two women. Today, Theresa and Jill laughingly tell you 'we've got away with it and you better keep your nose out of our business in future'.

Discuss: **Would you leave it at that or would you want to take it further?**

What would you do to take this matter further?

What do you think the manager should have done previously?

4 Handling Disclosure

No one knows where or when they might hear a disclosure about abuse and it often occurs when you least expect it. Therefore, it is crucial that anyone who might be the recipient of a disclosure should have training on how to behave appropriately. I always suggest to people that if they get the chance to do a short counselling course (even a 1 or 2 day course) then apply for it because those courses will offer very basic training on listening skills, responding and so on. This chapter will focus on *how* a worker should handle disclosure by considering how to:

- improve listening skills
- respond correctly
- be aware of body language (your own and the client's)
- follow through/take appropriate action.

LISTENING TO DISCLOSURE

We would all probably say that we are 'good at listening', but are we? What is good listening? It is important to give the client (here we are talking about a victim or maybe an abuser, because workers must not forget that they may have an abuser disclosing about what s/he has done) time to say everything s/he wants to say without butting in. The recipient of disclosure must never rush in and start bombarding the client with questions.

When a worker starts to hear disclosure there may be things to distract them from listening, that is, their own emotions. For example, they may be hearing things which trigger off their thoughts about their own bad experiences (abuse experienced in their own childhood; the worker may currently be living in an abusive marital situation). The worker can also have other reactions which result in being distracted:

- **irritation/anger**
  at what is being said or that s/he is having to listen to what is said

- **stereotype the victim/abuser**
  because of what the client is saying

- **not prepared to listen**
  due to fear of what s/he might hear and the responsibility s/he might have to take.

If the worker is distracted by any of these emotions s/he will not be able to listen fully and accurately. This is important because a worker will later have to record what has been said. Exercise 4.1 will help workers to develop their listening skills.

As well as listening to the victim it is important to watch for other messages. What is *not* being said? Workers must watch the victim's facial expressions and body language. Exercise 4.2. will help workers to think what emotions a victim of abuse may be feeling when they are disclosing about the abuse they have experienced, but also what the natural emotions are for a worker to feel. Just because we have to behave in a professional way does not mean that we do not *feel* anything. We are all human beings and it is very important that workers can vent their feelings somewhere. But in order to do this they have to realize what they may feel and that it is all right to have those feelings.

Workers need to think about their own:

- **Voice**

- **Eye contact**

- **Facial expressions**

- **Body**

Voice

When a worker is listening to disclosure s/he may be feeling all sorts of emotions and this can affect his/her voice. When any of us is shocked or surprised, our voices can become high pitched or we stutter. The worker must remain calm and endeavour to keep his/her voice as normal as possible. The worker needs to think about **tone, pitch, level,** and **inflection,** but also about the **spacing of words, the use of emphases, pauses** and **silences**. It is important to speak clearly and loud enough (especially if the client has a hearing loss) so that the client does not have to keep asking the worker to repeat what s/he said.

Eye Contact

It is important to give good eye contact to the client because it is an indication that the worker is listening. Seating arrangements are important; ideally the worker and the client should be sitting on the same level (although this is not always possible because of the seats available or because the client insists that the worker sits in a particular chair!). The worker needs to look away from time to time in order not to give the effect of **staring** at the client. If eye contact is constant, it can make the client feel uncomfortable.

Facial Expressions

I keep stressing that workers should not show that they are feeling shock, horror, disgust at what is being said. Emotions are shown in our faces so it is vital that a worker keeps a check on what their face is showing. This is *not* to say that a worker should keep a blank expression on his/her face throughout the disclosure. It is important to use the face to indicate that the client is being listened to and to show empathy and understanding.

Body

Body language is crucial; it can say as much as our faces! The worker should try to adopt a relaxed, open position. If arms and legs are crossed this is showing a barrier to the client. Whilst listening to the client, the worker should keep checking what is happening to the position of their own body because it will move and change, without the worker consciously realizing it. If the worker feels and looks comfortable, the client will feel more at ease whilst disclosing.

Again, to indicate the worker is listening, using the head is important. Nodding is a way of indicating that the worker is accepting the disclosure but also encouraging it. The intensity of nodding can indicate the level of agreement or acceptance. Leaning the head to one side can indicate to the client that the worker is listening intensely.

Hand movements/gestures can also be important in giving a sign of what the worker is feeling. However, the hands should not be used too much because it can distract the client from what s/he is saying. Hands should be used to indicate that the worker is receiving what is being said and drawing out more disclosure.

Breathing is another part of body language. It can be a good indicator of the level of tension. Again the worker should regularly check what is happening to his/her own breathing. Taking long deep breaths from the stomach are helpful to bring about feelings of calmness and the feelings of panic (which we all get when we suddenly realize we are hearing a disclosure!) will go away.

A victim or abuser will probably find it very difficult to talk about what has happened and s/he may feel very uncomfortable indeed. Consequently, the disclosure may come in fits and starts; it may not flow easily. The worker must allow for this by permitting silences to last a little longer than you would in normal conversation. It is at these points that workers usually want to rush in and fill the silences. Obviously if the disclosure seems to have come to a full stop it may be useful to use a prompt to check whether the client has finished. Handout 4.1 summarizes some simple rules for hearing disclosure.

RESPONDING TO DISCLOSURE

It is very important that the worker gets things right; that is, has s/he heard correctly, put the right interpretation on what has been said? In order to do this the worker must **reflect** back regularly what has been said through the disclosure, but also reflect back the perceived feelings of the client. This is important to check out whether the worker is hearing correctly but also to ensure that s/he can take the correct information back for recording purposes. Workers have to develop the skills of reflecting; they cannot be acquired overnight. It is important to reflect back correctly and at appropriate intervals. If the worker reflects back too frequently s/he will start to sound like a parrot and this may deter the client from disclosing further. Exercise 4.3 will help develop skills to reflect.

Sometimes workers have been in an abusive situation themselves and therefore can empathize with a victim. Even if a worker has not been in such a situation, s/he must try to imagine what the client is feeling (hence the reason for doing Exercise 4.2). Empathy has been defined as:

> 'It involves being sensitive, moment by moment, to the changing felt meanings which flow in the other person, to the fear or rage or tenderness or confusion or whatever that he or she is experiencing.' (Rogers 1980, p.142)

> 'an attempt to enter into another person's experience, and to feel and think as that person might' (Jacobs 1985, p.49)

Although it is important to listen and reflect back to the client, the worker will have to use questions at some point. Questions must be kept to a minimum or else the situation will turn into what feels like an interrogation. As Gerard Egan said 'When in doubt as to what to say or do, inept helpers tend to ask questions, as if amassing information were the goal of the helping interview' (Egan 1994, p.124). The discussion should never turn into a question and answer session. Probes and prompts are useful to get the client to reveal information, but they have to be followed up with empathy rather than a string of questions.

Questions must have a purpose; they are not there to fill a gap or awkward silence. When hearing disclosure about abuse, the worker is trying to find out what has happened and when.

There are two types of question which can be used – open and closed. Closed questions limit the response to 'yes', 'no' and other monosyllabic responses. Open ended questions give the client the opportunity to expand on what they are trying to say, how they are feeling and so on. However, the worker needs to ascertain what has happened to a client or what is happening to them now, so s/he needs to get **precise** information. This is when a **closed** question needs to be used.

The worker must **not** put words into the client's mouth, that is, s/he must not ask leading questions:

> 'Did your son hit you?'

> 'Did she take the money while you were watching television'

> 'Has Sharon been swearing at you again?

More useful questions would be:

> 'How did this happen?'

> 'What has happened?'

> 'When did this happen?'

> 'Who did this?'

> 'Where did this happen'

The word **why** must be avoided at all costs, because it can be very limiting. Again, it makes the client feel as if s/he is being interrogated. The use of 'why' can make the client feel that there has to be an explanation, when in fact there might not be. It can limit the client by not letting him/her talk about feelings and behaviours. When hearing disclosure it is not necessary to pursue why it has happened at this stage. Carrying out Exercise 4.4 will make workers realize just how awful it is to use the word 'why'.

During a disclosure a worker must try to get as much information about the incident or abusive situation as possible. Victims very often disclose once, then clam up because they regret having spoken. It may be a very long time (even years) before they talk about it again (if ever). The worker might be the only person to hear what has happened because the client refuses to discuss it with anyone else. We also have to remember that it is extremely difficult to find out what has happened to a victim who is confused. Therefore, a worker has to take advantage of the opportunity if a confused client does start talking about abuse and get as much information as possible.

The worker needs to ascertain when and where the abuse has happened. To do this questions might have to be asked about what the client was doing at the time. S/he may remember that s/he was watching a particular television programme or listening to a radio programme or eating breakfast or the district nurse had called that day when the abuse occurred. It is crucial to follow up these indicators to get factual information.

When it seems that the client has said everything they want to say, the worker must reflect back again and summarize everything that the client has said. This is why good listening skills are so crucial. A worker must be attentive all of the time or else s/he may miss a vital bit of information. Exercise 4.5 will help workers develop their skills in summarizing disclosures.

The worker must then ask the client what s/he wants to happen. Many victims will say they do not want the worker to do anything, because they just wanted to 'get it off my chest' or 'I just had to tell someone'. At this stage, the worker again has to remind the client about the boundaries of confidentiality and say that s/he will have to report what has been said to the line manager. It was emphasized in Chapter 3 that as soon as a worker starts to hear a disclosure s/he must remind the client that s/he may have to report this back to the line manager. If the client does want some help/intervention, the worker must make it very clear what action she is going to take next.

Throughout any interview the worker must remain calm and not show the emotions s/he may be feeling (remember Exercise 4.2). Some typical emotions when hearing about abuse may be: surprise, shock, horror, disgust.

Finally, Exercise 4.6 is to make participants think about what they would actually say in certain situations. Before carrying out the exercise the two Handouts 4.6(a) and 4.6(b) should be given out and discussed. These lay the foundation for developing good practice.

Suggested Reading

Many good books on counselling now exist and trainers may wish to use materials from some of them to develop ideas and materials about basic counselling skills. Particularly good series are:

Counselling in Action – Series Editor: Windy Dryden. Published by Sage.

Counselling in Context – Series Editors: Moira Walker and Michael Jacobs. Published by Open University Press.

Dryden, W., Charles-Edwards, D. and Woolfe, R. (1989) *Handbook of Counselling in Britain*. London: Tavistock/Routledge.

Egan, G. (1994) *The Skilled Helper*, 5th edition. Pacific Grove, Ca: Brooks/Cole Publishing Company.

Jacobs, M. (1985) *Swift to Hear*. London: SPCK.

Mattinson, J. (1975) *The Reflection Process in Casework Supervision.* London: Institute of Marital Studies.

Nelson-Jones, R. (1983) *Practical Counselling and Helping Skills.* London: Cassell.

Rogers, C.R. (1980) *A Way of Being.* Boston: Houghton Mifflin.

Some Simple Rules for Hearing Disclosure

- Let the client speak

- Listen

- Do not be distracted by your own feelings/emotions

- Do not rush in with a comment/interrupt

- Do not bombard the client with questions

- Remember as much as you can

- Watch for non verbal clues

- Feel comfortable with silences

LISTENING SKILLS

Objective

To improve a worker's listening skills

Participants

Exercise to be carried out in pairs

Equipment

None

Time

20 minutes

Task

Participants are asked to think for one minute about a situation/incident in their lives which made them feel really scared/frightened.

One participant will then go first and talk for 5 minutes in great detail about what happened and how they felt. The other participant will listen and is not allowed to say anything (i.e. no comments or questions) except 'mm' or 'yes'.

After 5 minutes the participants will swop, and the other participant will tell his/her story.

The participants will then feedback what it was like to be in the different roles, i.e. of speaker, of listener.

EMOTIONS

Objective

To make participant think about which emotions a victim may be experiencing when disclosing about abuse.

Participants

To be done individually

Equipment

Paper and pen

Time

5 minutes to make list

15 minutes for feedback and discussion in a large group

Task

To make a list of emotions which a victim may be feeling when talking about an abusive situation.

NOTE: this exercise should be repeated asking:

(1) **which emotions an abuser may experience when disclosing**

(2) **which emotions a worker may experience whilst listening to disclosure**

REFLECTING

Objective

To develop skills in reflecting back what has been said

Participants

To work in pairs

Equipment

Role plays to have been written on cards

Time

5 minutes to role play

5 minutes to feedback.

Task

The two participants engage in a role play. Whoever is in role as a worker should reflect back what has been said at appropriate intervals.

Feedback

In pairs discuss what happened; that is, what it felt like to be reflecting back and how it felt to hear the reflection.

(Chapter 11 includes role plays which can be adapted for this exercise)

THE WHY? QUESTION

Objective

To make participants realize how limiting the word 'why' is when asking questions

Participants

To work in pairs

Equipment

Role plays to have been written on cards

Time

5 minutes to role play

5 minutes to feedback.

Task

Participants engage in role play, but the participant who is the worker can only use the word 'why' throughout the interview.

Feedback

Participants discuss how it felt for them both during the role play.

Stage 2

Participants are then given the handout 'Some useful words' to read. Participants then repeat the same the role play. The worker is to ask questions using these words rather than why questions.

(Chapter 11 includes role plays which can be adapted for this exercise)

Some Useful Words

HOW?

WHO?

WHAT?

WHEN?

WHERE?

SUMMARIZING A DISCLOSURE

Objective

To develop skills in summarizing what has been said during a disclosure

Participants

To work in pairs

Equipment

Role plays to have been written on cards

Time

5 minutes to role play

5 minutes for the person in the role of worker to summarize

5 minutes for general feedback

Task

The two participants engage in a role play. At the end of the role play the worker will summarize what has been said by the client.

Feedback

In pairs discuss what happened; that is, did the worker summarize what had been said correctly and how did it feel (1) repeating what had been said (2) hearing what had been said?

(Chapter 11 includes role plays which can be adapted for this exercise)

WHAT WOULD YOU SAY IF...?

Objective

To make participants think about how they would react if they found themselves in a certain situation.

Participants

Exercise to be carried out in small groups

Equipment

Handouts to be photocopied beforehand

Flipchart paper and pens

Time

30 minutes to complete the exercise

Task

Participants are asked to consider and discuss in their groups each scenario in turn and write down the actual *words* they would *say* if they found themselves in that situation.

Some examples are given below in the handout below. Some of these situations could occur either in the community or in a residential setting.

Exercise
What Would You Say If...?

1. A husband says to you 'She hits me all the time, but please don't tell anyone'.

2. A confused client says her son raped her last night.

3. A colleague tells you that she hit a client last week because she had reached the end of her tether.

4. A client says to you 'I'm starving. My son doesn't feed me'.

5. A client tells you she thinks her home help is not giving her enough change from the shopping each week.

6. Brenda says to you: 'It's a terrible thing to admit but I am scared of my own grandchildren, but I can't tell you why because it will make it worse'.

7. 'It's my own fault he gets cross with me. I'm too much for him. I should have died years ago'.

8. Mrs Bell is convinced that her neighbour is giving her too much medication.

9. Edgar gets confused sometimes. Today he says £20 has gone missing from under the vase which is on top of the television.

10. Mrs Dixon says her daughter makes her sleep on the kitchen floor.

Don'ts

- Laugh

- Joke about what has been said

- Ignore what you have been told

- Dismiss what you have heard

- Change the subject

- Say things like: 'Don't be stupid'

                                      'That's ridiculous'

                                      'Come off it'

                                      'Stop messing'

                                      'You're joking'

                                      'Pull the other one'

                                      'S/he wouldn't do that'

You Must

- Take what you have been told seriously – even if the person is confused

- Talk to the client some more without interrogating him/her

- Ascertain the facts – what has happened and when

- Ask the client what s/he wants to do

- Remind the client about the boundaries of confidentiality

- Report to your manager

5 Monitoring and Reviewing

A frequently used cliche in social care work is 'we'll monitor the situation', but what does it mean? It makes people feel better because they think they are 'doing' something, but what are they doing? If we are going to monitor elder abuse cases it must be done thoroughly and systematically. People need to know *how* they are going to monitor, and what monitoring tools will be used.

A manager may say to a worker that s/he has not got enough evidence to refer the case on for a formal elder abuse investigation, so s/he is to monitor the situation for a bit longer. Workers must write down what they monitor, but they need to know *where* to write it down. Systems for home care staff vary considerably. Some home care staff carry notebooks/diaries around with them, others 'just have to tell my manager; she writes it down'. Workers need to be clear about what files are kept and where. The same applies in residential/day care settings – where should concerns be written down – in the log book or in the resident/user's file?

RECORDING

Accurate recording of what has happened is crucial. Workers must record the facts, that is:

- o **what has been said**

- o **what has happened**

- o **where**

- o **when**

Workers should not speculate about what may have happened or write anything about their own personal feelings. This is because such notes can be used at a later date as evidence in a court of law and the defence barrister could use such notes to the abuser's advantage.

When recording what has been said or what has happened it is important to put a date on the record. If a client discloses about something which has happened it is useful to state the time the disclosure took place.

Some workers are 'not very good at writing' and I am aware that some workers cannot read or write and they keep this fact a secret. Therefore, it is important that some attention is given to recording in training sessions. Time needs to be spent on what it is appropriate to record and how to do it. Even minor concerns could become important and relevant later on. Exercise 5.1 will help workers to think through what they should be recording and how to record the facts clearly.

MONITORING TOOLS

Monitoring tools are a way of recording what is happening and therefore can take different forms. Let us think about physical abuse in the first instance. A worker may suspect that a client is being physically abused, but the client denies it and always has a very good excuse about how s/he has got an injury, for example:

'I fell out of bed'

'I walked into the door'

'I burnt myself on the saucepan'

In these circumstances, the worker needs to keep a record of how often these injuries are occurring and this can be done with the use of bodycharts. A typical bodychart is shown in Figure 5.1.

Something which workers may find difficult is the fact that you have to be honest with the client if you are going to use the bodycharts as a way of recording. It has to be explained to the client that you have concerns and are worried about them. The client should know that records are kept as normal procedure, so using a bodychart is just another way of adding to the records. This needs to be explained very simply and clearly to the client.

The bodychart is very simple to use and can be used by home care staff who are working with people in the community, day centre staff who may have worries about a user in their centre and residential staff for their own own residents but also for people coming in for respite care. When an injury is seen it is drawn onto the bodychart (and you do not have to be a Van Gogh to do this!) and a small description is written about the injury:

Some examples

'the bruise was round and about 2 centimetres in diameter. It was on Mrs X's left cheek. It was very dark brown'

'Bernard had a large cut from his elbow down to his little finger. Pus was coming out of it. It looked infected. It had not been covered up'

'Miss P had two black eyes and her chin was all bruised underneath. She told me she had fallen down the stairs'

'I saw bruises behind both ears. Blue and purple'.

The date the injury(ies) was seen and by whom must be written at the top of the bodychart and then placed in the client's file. Sometimes it is amazing how many charts are completed. They can be used as a basis for discussion in supervision sessions, because they help the worker to focus on what has been happening and just how often. Workers who work with a large number of people often find it difficult to remember exactly how many charts are filled in for one particular client

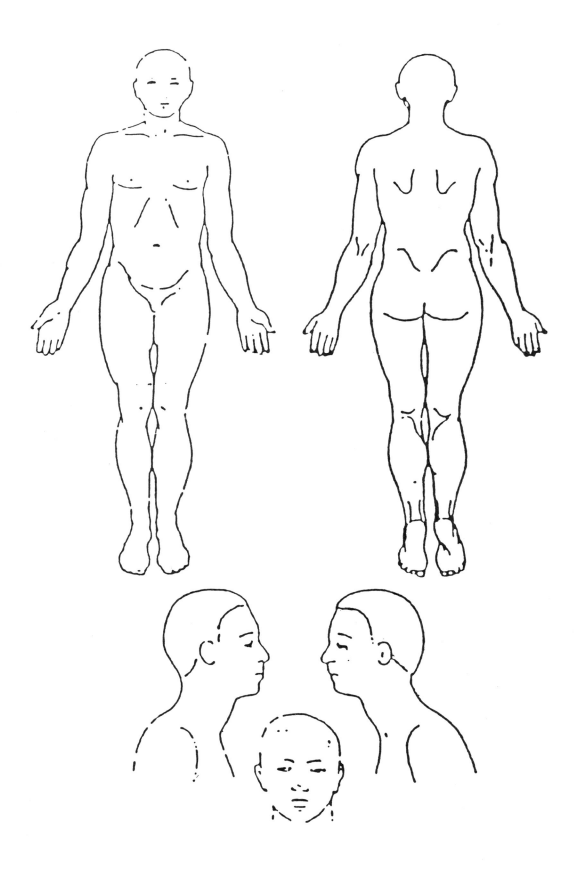

Figure 5.1

and will be surprised when they look at the file during supervision. Exercise 5.2 will help workers practise using bodycharts.

More monitoring tools need to be designed specifically for working with cases of elder abuse and the different types of abuse, not just physical abuse. So far we have inherited assessment tools from America and Canada (see Davies 1993; Fulmer 1984: Ross *et al.* 1985). Tools can be very simple and workers can design their own. A basic question needs to be asked 'What are you trying to monitor?' and then discuss how you are going to do it.

SOME EXAMPLES

A home care assistant, Sue, is worried about Emily, who suffers from Alzheimer's Disease, because she is losing so much weight. The GP has examined her and carried out various blood tests; there is nothing physically wrong with her. Sue suspects that Emily's daughter is not feeding her properly in the evenings. Sue has got a little book where she keeps a daily record of what is in the fridge and what she prepares for Emily to eat at lunchtime. She has also agreed with her home care manager that she will sit and chat to Emily whilst she is eating to see how much she does eat or leave. Sue also weighs Emily once a week.

Fred likes the volunteer who visits him in the old people's home every week, because he has no family or friends. However, Fred has started saying that money is going missing from his room. He is not making any direct accusations, but staff are worried that at some point he is going to accuse one of them. The principal and Fred's keyworker have talked about the problem with Fred and discussed the fact that anyone could be taking the money (staff, another resident, a visitor). Fred himself thinks it is the volunteer. With Fred's agreement, a senior member of staff will check with Fred every morning and every evening how much cash Fred has in his wallet. The amounts will be written down on a special sheet to be kept in Fred's file. When money goes missing, a check will be done on who has been in the room, in the unit that day etc.

In some authorities special forms have been designed for monitoring purposes. Figure 5.2 shows the form which is currently being used in Calderdale Social Services by home care staff for monitoring.

REVIEWING

It is no good monitoring a situation unless you review it at regular intervals. If a case conference has taken place, then a date should be set to reconvene and review the protection plan if there is one (see Chapters 6 and 7). However, if a formal elder abuse investigation has not taken place, a worker's manager needs to regularly review the case in supervision.

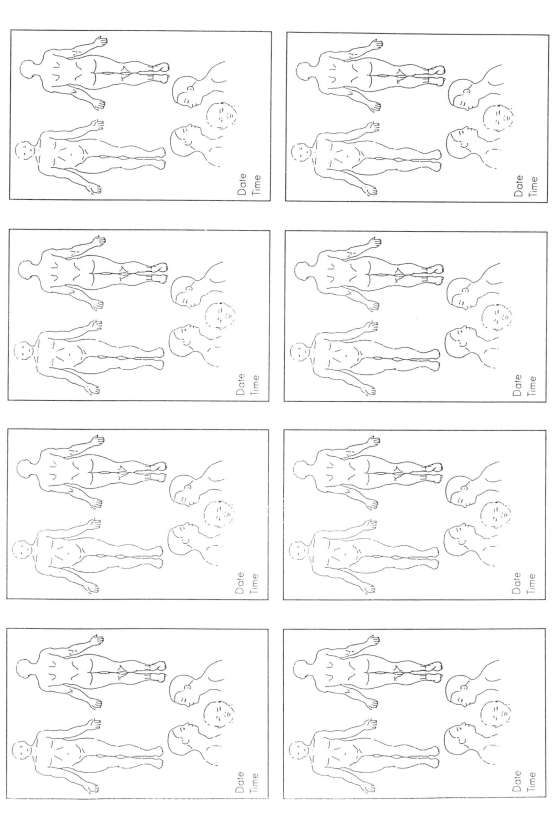

Reproduced by permission of Calderdale Social Services Department

Figure 5.2

Client Concern Record

Client's Number ....

Home Care Assistant's Name ....

	Date	Time	Cause for Concern	Manager Informed	Date
1					
2					
3					
4					
5					
6					
7					
8					
9					
10					
11					
12					
13					
14					

'Causes for Concern' might be things like...... bruises on back; unusually quiet; not enough food in cupboards; said she was hungry; looked frightened; said he didn't like his son coming; asked me not to bath her; ......always say **what** happened, not **why** you think they happened. If you notice any injuries, mark them on the charts on the back of this sheet.

Reproduced by permission of Calderdale Social Services Department

Figure 5.2

SUGGESTED READING

Trainers should check whether there are any specific monitoring forms being used in their own Department or in the local Health Authority.

Davies, M. (1993) 'Recognizing abuse: an assessment tool for nurses.' In P. Decalmer and F. Glendenning (eds) *The Mistreatment of Elderly People.* London: Sage, Chapter 6.

Fulmer, T. (1984) 'Elder abuse assessment tool.' *Dimensions of Critical Care Nursing 3*, 4, 216–220.

Ross, M., Ross, P.A, and Ross, M.C. (February 1985) 'Abuse of the elderly.' *The Canadian Nurse 81*, 36–39.

RECORDING CONVERSATIONS

Objective

To help participants improve their written recording of conversation, disclosure, interviews.

Participants

To work on their own

Equipment

Pens and paper

Preparation needed by trainer

The trainer needs to find a video which will show an interview(s) or part of a conversation. If such a video is not available, a role play should be simulated and watched.

Time

To show an interview/role play

Appropriate time for participants to write their record (depending on the length of the interview/role play)

Feedback in groups

Task

Participants watch an interview/role play. They are asked to consider the important bits which need to be recorded. They then write the record.

Feedback

Participants share their records in groups of four. The trainer goes round each group to check on what has been written.

USE OF BODYCHARTS

Objective

To help participants get used to using bodycharts

Participants

To work on their own

Equipment

Bodycharts

Pens

Time

5 minutes

Task

Participants are shown a photograph/slide of some injuries on a person's body. Participants then have to draw the injuries on the bodychart and write a description of what they saw.

Feedback

Participants compare their bodycharts

6 Case Conferences Made Simple

If they are honest enough to admit it, everyone has a fear of case conferences. The fear can arise for a number of reasons, for example previous bad experiences or fear of the unknown. Very few professionals receive training on case conferences, so others who also have to attend are even less likely to know what to expect. All managers should prepare their workers for a case conference if they do not know what to expect or if s/he has had little experience. This chapter is written with the objective that it may help both home care staff and staff working in residential settings and day centres to increase their confidence in presenting information at case conferences.

There are some things which need to be borne in mind throughout any training session or discussion on case conferences:

dealing with elder abuse is different from child abuse – there are no statutory powers, so this can affect outcomes/interventions

even if a worker has some experience in child protection work s/he needs to reflect on:

- **procedures**

- **his/her own practices and behaviour at conferences**

- **transferring skills**

- **possible problems which may arise in elder abuse case conferences.**

SO WHY HAVE A CASE CONFERENCE?

Many people think that case conferences are a waste of valuable time. This is not true if they are conducted in a proper manner. A case conference brings people together to share their views and to discuss their work. It should be a forum where people can discuss their concerns, vent their feelings and anxieties and support each other. It is also a tool for organizing future intervention. In summary the main purposes of a case conference are to:

- exchange information in a multi disciplinary forum
- assess the client's situation and the degree of risk
- make decisions and recommendations which are to be implemented.

As well as a lot of debate about the usefulness of case conferences in recent years, there has also been much discussion about terminology. Guidelines on working with elder abuse use many different terms – for example case meeting, case discussion, planning meeting, case review meeting and so on. In this chapter I shall be using the term **case conference**.

Everyone who is present at the case conference needs to know why they are there and what the purposes of the conference are. If this is not clarified at an early stage then conferences will drift. A strong chairperson who knows what s/he is doing is crucial in facilitating the flow of the conference.

People are always saying that they 'have not got time' to do certain things and one of these 'things' is allocating time to prepare for a case conference. My response is 'you make time' if you want to do your job well. The philosophy 'you can learn by doing' is acceptable in some areas of work, but when a worker is contributing to a discussion about possible elder abuse, then it is not acceptable to learn as you go along. *All* workers need to be prepared. If training departments do not provide case conference training, then managers can help the worker in supervision sessions, allocating extra time to the worker before a case conference takes place, or discussing the whole issue of case conferences in a team meeting.

TASKS

Participants attending a case conference have several tasks to perform, namely:

(1) TO GIVE AND SHARE INFORMATION

The information given must be accurate. The participant gives factual information about the people they know (victim, abuser, other important personnel). Obviously, participants voice their concerns, but they must also highlight the strengths of a situation not just the negatives (e.g. the feelings of the victim).

Any gaps in information should always be identified and acknowledged. Workers should not feel inadequate if they do not have certain information available or they just do not know something. If information is lacking and can be obtained at a future date, it may be necessary to reconvene the case conference.

(2) TO ASSESS THE LEVEL OF RISK

For years we have bandied the term 'at risk' about and now it is becoming more important because of the developments in risk assessment and risk management work (see Kemshall and Pritchard 1995). Everyone needs to be clear about risk assessment. Some useful points for discussion in training sessions are:

- **What does risk assessment mean?**

- o **What are the principles and criteria?**

- o **Are we all working towards the same ends?**

- o **Do other professionals/people understand what we mean?**

- o **Does the victim (who may be present at the case conference) know what risk assessment means?**

- o **What does risk mean to him/her?**

- o **How do we predict risk?**

(3) DECIDE ON REGISTRATION (IF A REGISTER EXISTS)

Few authorities have 'at risk' registers for adults. Where they do exist conference participants must know what the defined criteria are for putting a person's name on the register.

(4) CO-ORDINATE FUTURE INTERVENTION

This will involve the formulation of a protection plan, which will state the tasks and responsibilities of everyone who will be involved. The keyworker will be responsible for ensuring that the plan is implemented and reconvening the case conference if there are difficulties in implementing the plan; for example, a worker is not undertaking the tasks s/he agreed to do.

PREPARATION

Workers need to know what is expected of them at a case conference and from my experience, very few home care staff and residential/day care workers know what is going to happen at the conference or what they are going to be asked. Handout 6.1 shows a list of questions which may help a manager and worker to focus on preparing for a case conference.

It is crucial that the worker has time to think about what they know about the case and what information may be useful. A worker also needs to be told what sort of information is *not* useful (for example, graphic detail about the furniture, colour of the curtains may not be relevant). If a participant waffles on about irrelevant things, other contributors may stop listening and miss other relevant information.

I always suggest that workers make a list of key points they want to make and write them down on a very small bit of paper, which they can keep at the side of them during the conference. I have always found this a useful thing to do, because when you are nervous you forget things. Many workers have told me that they have felt sick throughout the case conference and have been too scared to speak, never mind remember what they wanted to say!

It is helpful for a worker to discuss what they want to say, but they also need to practice. S/he can do this by role playing or what may be less embarrassing is practising alone in front of a mirror. After preparing the information, the worker should sit in front of a mirror and present the information. It is crucial to speak *clearly, slowly and loud enough*. There is nothing worse than a chairperson asking a participant to repeat what s/he has just said. The participant gets embarrassed and probably talks even faster when repeating the information (just to get it over with!). A useful tip is to talk slower than normal and if you sound as if you are talking too slowly you are probably talking at about the right speed.

WHAT SHOULD HAPPEN AT A CASE CONFERENCE?

I said before that a worker should know what is going to happen at a case conference. This is not only important for the worker, but maybe the worker will have to help prepare a client/victim if s/he is going to attend the conference as well. Most chairpeople tend to follow an agenda. Handout 6.2 illustrates a typical agenda.

The chairperson asks everyone to present information they have available for the conference. It is important that people present facts and do not speculate. Information should be presented in a concise manner. This is why it was stressed above that workers *must* prepare for case conferences.

Workers who do not have much experience of attending case conferences often see it as an ordeal. They may dread the fact that they are going to have to speak at all. Many of them will feel intimidated by the people they see as more experienced (for example the social workers who attend case conferences 'all the time') and the people who are considered to have more status (for example the 'posh consultant who talks proper').

THE ISSUE OF JARGON

We all use jargon at some point in our working lives. We use it without thinking and perhaps not realizing that to other people it is jargon. However, at case conferences jargon needs to be avoided. It can often baffle and confuse people, especially a victim who is attending a conference. So what is jargon? Exercise 6.1 will help workers to think about the jargon they use at work, but also what they have heard elsewhere (and perhaps not understood)

Group dynamics are very important in a case conference. Some people will feel that they have power, others will feel totally powerless and believe they cannot influence any decision. During a case conference it is necessary to listen to all participants, but also to watch their facial expressions and body language. Participants need to think about how they can present their information and arguments assertively and convincingly. Certain individuals may dominate the discussion. The chairperson *should* intervene but sometimes this does not happen. Therefore, all participants should give some thought to how they might tackle some difficult people/situations at case conferences. Exercise 6.2 will help to do this.

There are lots of things to think about when you are going to attend a case conference and another helpful way to prepare for the experience is to simulate a case conference and then analyze what happened. Before the case conference exercise is undertaken participants should be given the 'do's and dont's' checklists which are shown in handouts 6.3(a) and 6.3(b)

SUGGESTED READING

In order to read anything worthwhile about case conferences it is necessary to turn to the literature on child abuse. Some useful references are:

Hallet, C. and Stevenson, O. (1980) 'Case conferences – their background and purposes' and Chapter 4 'Case conferences – the processes.' In *Child Abuse: Aspects of Interprofessional Co-operation*. London: George Allen and Unwin, Chapter 3.

Charles, M. (1993) 'Child protection conferences: maximising their potential.' In H. Owen and J. Pritchard (eds) *Good Practice in Child Protection*. London: Jessica Kingsley.

Corby, B. (1993) *Child Abuse: Towards a Knowledge Base*. Buckingham: Open University Press.

Corby, B. (1987) *Working with Child Abuse*. Milton Keynes: Open University Press.

Kemshall, H. and Pritchard, J. (1995) *Good Practice in Risk Assessment and Risk Management*. London: Jessica Kingsley.

Preparation for Participants

- Who is likely to be at the case conference?

- Check the date, time, venue – have I got it right?

- What information is needed?

- What do I know about the client, situation etc?

- What more do I need to know?

- Are my notes/case file up to date and in order?

- What do I want to say?

- Whose views am I representing (e.g. my own, the client's, the agency's)?

- Make a list of key points (up to 10) I want to make

- What are my true feelings about this case?

Case Conference Agenda
What Should Happen

- Introductions

- Clarify details of the subject

- Explanation about reasons for convening the case conference

- Reminder about confidentiality

- Findings of the initial investigation

- Each participant will talk about their involvement with or knowledge of the subject/abuser/other relevant people

- Full discussion

- Decision about registration (if applicable)

- Recommendations

- Formulation of protection plan

- Date of next conference.

© Jacki Pritchard, 1996

Useful Tips: Do's

- Prepare yourself

- Arrive on time

- Sit properly

- Think before you speak

- Speak clearly, slowly and loud enough

- Present the facts/accurate information

- Have information readily available

- Be professional

- Be ready to challenge/disagree

Useful Tips: Don'ts

- Slouch

- Mumble/waffle on

- Use jargon

- Jump to conclusions

- Be judgemental

- Get angry/upset

- Be intimidated

WHAT JARGON DO I KNOW?

Objective

We sometimes forget that we ourselves use jargon because we are so used to words/clichés. This exercise will help workers realize what jargon exists in all professions.

Participants

Participants to work individually

Equipment

Sheet of paper, pen, blutack

Time

5 minutes to make personal list.

5 minutes to read other lists.

10 minutes for general discussion.

Task

Each participant is to make a list of jargon they use themselves, they have heard at a case conference/discussion or they hear in their workplace (by colleagues and other professionals). Participants should write jargon they have heard, even if they do not know what it means. All lists are then pinned up on a wall. Participants are to read the lists and to ask if they do not know the meaning of any jargon.

DEALING WITH PEOPLE AT CASE CONFERENCES

Objective

To make participants think about difficult behaviour at case conferences and how they would deal with the person/problem.

Participants

Exercise to be carried out in small groups (4–5 people)

Equipment

Flipchart paper and pens

Time

Groups are given 10 minutes to work on each problem. The trainer is to decide how many problems will be worked upon. The flipcharts are then pinned up and discussed in a large group.

Task

A group has to consider what they would do or say if they encountered a situation in a case conference. They must assume that the chairperson does not intervene. Exact words and sentences must be written down on the flipchart sheet.

When the large group discussion takes place participants should say why they think some statements are good and why they would not use others themselves.

Preparation

The trainer will write one problem/behaviour on the top of a flipchart sheet for each group. Some examples are given in the following handout.

Examples of Difficult People/situations

- A GP says 'She suffering from dementia. How can you believe anything she says?'

- How do you stop a person butting in?

- Someone keeps repeating the same thing over and over again

- You do not understand what someone is trying to say

- You have to admit that you do not the know the meaning of a word or piece of jargon

- How do you encourage someone to speak (because you know they have some important/vital information) without making them feel they are being put on the spot?

- A policeman says 'It is a waste of time being here. People with learning difficulties are useless at giving statements and evidence'

- How do you stop someone from dominating the conference?

- One professional says to you 'You are talking a load of rubbish'

- You want to speak but everyone keeps getting in before you

- The chairperson ignores you when you try to speak

- The victim (your client) refuses to talk because s/he is either upset or angry

- You want to tell someone that you find their comment offensive

CASE CONFERENCE

Objective

To convene a case conference in order to give participants the opportunity to practice and learn through role play.

Participants

Large group

Equipment

Large table and chairs

Information sheets to be prepared beforehand by the trainer

Roles to be prepared beforehand by the trainer

Lists of attenders

Name labels for participants to wear

Time

Participants should have 10 minutes to read the information sheet and their role sheet

The case conference will run for 30 minutes

Feedback/analysis 25 minutes

Task

To convene the case conference

Feedback

The trainer should ask the following questions: How did it feel? What was good/bad? What would you do differently? What did you learn from that experience? What did the trainer/observers see/hear? Who was powerful? Why?

SIMULATION EXERCISE I

Background Information
(to be given to all participants)

SUBJECT: Ruth Michaels

AGE: 72

Ruth Michaels lives alone in a very large Victorian house. She loves the house because she was born in it and lived there with her husband, Robert, until he died ten years ago. Ruth has four children – three daughters who all live away and rarely visit – and one son, Luke, who lives locally.

The house has fallen into disrepair because Ruth has very little money. Robert left her well off when he died, but five years ago Luke persuaded his mother to lend him a large amount of money to set up his own business. He has never paid the money back and has borrowed more from her whenever the business has been in trouble. He also persuaded her to put her bank account into joint names, so he could 'worry about the finances'. Luke keeps the cheque book and has the bank statements sent to his home. He has now told his mother that she 'must sell the house to save the business'.

Home care staff have been very worried about Ruth for sometime. They go in twice a day to check on her, prepare lunch and tea, and shop once a week. They are convinced that Luke is financially abusing his mother on a regular basis. A district nurse currently visits to dress Ruth's leg ulcers.

A social worker became involved after home care staff referred Ruth for a full needs assessment. The social worker has talked to Ruth about the abuse she is experiencing, but Ruth says she does not want anyone to speak to Luke about money or her situation. She understands why people are concerned about her and has agreed to come to the case conference today on the condition that Luke is not told about it.

List of Attenders

Chairperson
Ruth
Social worker
Home care staff x 2
District nurse
GP
Principal, old people's home
Day centre worker
Bank Manager

ROLE: CHAIRPERSON

You are to chair the case conference

ROLE: RUTH

You are very grateful to the people who are trying to help you and value their advice, but you are really frightened of your son and this is hindering your actions. You really want to stay in your house and die there when the time comes. The only reason you will consider selling the house is to help Luke. You love your son (who was born when you were 45 years old and is your favourite child) even though you have become scared of him since he has started hitting you and you know he is taking your pension money.

This is the reason why there is never enough money to buy food, new clothes or things you would like. You feel it is your duty to protect him. You have been to look round a local old people's home and day centre with the social worker and they all seemed like nice people. You have asked for your bank manager to be present today, so you can find out exactly how much money you have left, because Luke will never tell you anything.

ROLE: SOCIAL WORKER

You were allocated Ruth's case for a full needs assessment. You have visited Ruth about six times and are very concerned about her. From what Ruth has said she is definitely being financially abused by her son, but does not want any action taken. You are even more concerned about the physical neglect she is being subjected to and you feel she is very much at risk. You have talked to Ruth about residential care, but she realizes that the house would have to be sold to pay for her care. She does not really want to sell the house and would only do so to help Luke.

— —

ROLE: HOME CARE STAFF X 2

You have known Ruth for years now and think she is a wonderful person, but she has gone into a terrible decline during the two years. She has become very unkempt and rarely changes her clothes, whereas before she was always took pride in her appearance. She seems to have lost her appetite and says 'she does not want to eat', whereas before she loved her food and ate very heartily. On occasions there has been no money in the house for shopping and you have had to buy basic food to keep her going using your own money.

— —

ROLE: DISTRICT NURSE

You see Ruth three times a week to dress her leg ulcers. You are extremely concerned about her physical condition. She is very thin and continues to lose weight. Her skin is in very bad condition and her basic hygiene is not good. You have talked to Ruth about good diet and nutrition, but she says she just does not feel like eating any more.

ROLE: GENERAL PRACTITIONER

You have known Ruth and her family for many years. You can talk about how devoted Ruth is to her son, Luke. Luke was an 'accident' who was born when Ruth was 45 years old. It was clear that Ruth always favoured Luke and her three daughters resented this. You do not like Luke and think he is a 'spoilt brat'. You have been visiting Ruth quite regularly recently because of the concerns expressed by the district nurse and home care staff. You think Ruth would be better off going into residential care.

ROLE: PRINCIPAL, OLD PEOPLE'S HOME

The social worker brought Ruth to have a look round your home. You think Ruth would fit in well if she decided she wanted to go into residential care. If she is to remain at home, you can offer her some respite care.

ROLE: DAY CENTRE WORKER

The social worker brought Ruth to look round the old people's home where the day centre takes place. Ruth also spent some time in the day centre, because if she remains at home she may wish to attend a day centre. You think this would be good for her so that she could meet people but also you feel sure you could persuade her to eat more.

ROLE: BANK MANAGER

A social worker contacted you to come to this meeting, which you feel is very irregular and does not fit in with your usual schedule. Also you do not think it is right that Mr Michaels does not know about this meeting and you do not understand why everyone is making so much of 'keeping confidentiality' for Mrs Michaels' sake. You feel that Mr Michaels should be here as the account is in joint names. There is only £998 left in the bank account.

© Jacki Pritchard, 1996

✓

Background Information
(to be given to all participants)

SUBJECTS: Beatrice Caywood (age 79)
             Isabella Jepson (age 76)

Two sisters, Beatrice and Isabella, have lived together for many years now. They are both housebound. Beatrice suffered a stroke several years ago and can only walk a little way with a zimmer frame. Isabella is an amputee (she lost her leg in the Second World War) and in the past she has been agoraphobic. She only likes to go out to places where she feels safe.

The two sisters cope very well with the help of home care services. They go to day centre twice a week and have respite care at a local authority home (to which the day centre is attached). Beatrice's son, Alexander, is also involved with the care of the sisters. He visits them three times a week and handles all their financial affairs. There are no other living relatives.

Six months ago, day centre staff became concerned because Isabella seemed very quiet and withdrawn. She also burst into tears on several occasions. She said nothing was wrong. Residential staff also became concerned because on each respite stay the sisters had bruises on their arms and legs. They both claimed to have had falls. They have always refused to have the GP in to check their injuries.

Things came to a head two weeks ago when Isabella came to day centre on her own, because Beatrice had 'flu. Isabella had a black eye and bruising on her cheek. She disclosed to day centre staff that Alexander had hit her because she would not give him a cheque. Isabella said that he had been violent for a long time and it happens whenever the sisters refuse to give him money from their bank and building society accounts.

An elder abuse investigation has now taken place. Isabella wants something done to stop Alexander threatening her and Beatrice, but she does not want the police involved. Beatrice is still denying the abuse and is not talking to Isabella because of what she has told staff and blames her for the investigation taking place.

© Jacki Pritchard, 1996

List of attenders

Chairperson
Beatrice Caywood
Isabella Jepson
Social worker
Home care assistant
Home care organizer
Principal of the old people's home
Care assistant
Day centre staff x 2

- -

ROLE: CHAIRPERSON

You are to chair the case conference

- -

ROLE: BEATRICE CAYWOOD

You are extremely angry that this case conference is taking place
and you will ignore your sister completely. Throughout the conference you will deny that Alexander is violent and that he has hit
you. You will also deny that he has ever asked you and your sister
for money. You will claim that Isabella is just trying to cause trouble,
because she has never liked Alexander.

- -

ROLE: ISABELLA JEPSON

You are very nervous about attending the case conference and also
distressed that you have upset your sister, who dotes on her son.
However, you have reached the point where you believe that
something must be done to stop Alexander being physically violent
and forcing you to give him money. You are extremely frightened
of him, but will talk about all the times he has hit you and Beatrice.
However, you are adamant that you do not want the police involved, as you do not want Alexander being sent to prison. You
might consider going into residential care permanently.

ROLE: SOCIAL WORKER

You have been the investigating officer in this elder abuse investigation. You have interviewed the two sisters separately on several occasions. Isabella has disclosed about the physical and financial abuse the sisters have experienced from Alexander. Isabella wants it to stop but does not want the police involved. You think Isabella might consider going into residential care permanently. Beatrice has denied the abuse and is very angry with her sister, who she says is deliberately causing trouble.

ROLE: HOME CARE ASSISTANT

You go in three times a day to help the sisters and check that they are all right. You know Alexander quite well and do not like him at all. He is arrogant and always talks down to you. You have suspected for a long time that he abuses his mother and aunt, but they cover up for him. Whenever you have asked him for money to buy them clothes and things they need, he is reluctant to give you any money to go shopping. The sisters have sometimes gone without things that they really need.

ROLE: HOME CARE ORGANIZER

Today you are accompanying a home care assistant to a case conference to support her.

ROLE: PRINCIPAL, OLD PEOPLE'S HOME

You have known Beatrice and Isabella ever since they started coming in for respite care. You and members of staff have been concerned about the number of injuries they have had – mainly black eyes and bruises on different parts of their bodies. Staff have been keeping bodycharts of the injuries. Unfortunately, you have *not* told the sisters you have been doing this.

ROLE: CARE ASSISTANT

You have a really good relationship with Beatrice and Isabella and can talk to them about all sorts of things. You have done a lot of work with Isabella, talking about her agoraphobia and working with her to become more assertive. You feel this is the reason why she is now disclosing about the abuse from Alexander. She has told you since the investigation started that he has been abusing her and Beatrice for years.

- -

ROLE: DAY CENTRE STAFF X 2

You have liaised very closely with the residential staff, because you also have had concerns about the two sisters. Beatrice seems to be the dominant sister who bosses Isabella about, but gradually Isabella has become more assertive. Beatrice does not like the attention that her sister gets.

7 Long Term Work with Victims and Abusers

Throughout this book I have been establishing the fact that elder abuse is often well hidden and, therefore, very difficult to identify. A further difficulty is that the majority of victims choose to stay in the abusive situation. All this makes it very frustrating for anyone working closely with a victim.

Sometimes workers turn their backs on abusive situations because they believe that nothing can be done. This is the wrong attitude to have, because positive work can be undertaken to support a victim even if they choose to remain in the abusive situation. At times all the worker can do is to support someone in their decision. It may take years rather than weeks or months for a victim to choose to change the situation s/he is in.

It is very natural for any worker to want to protect a victim; it is a natural human instinct. It is very necessary to remind oneself continuously that elder abuse victims are adults and they have choices. We cannot make decisions for them, because we do not have any statutory powers.

Consequently, it is very important to develop strategies and ways of working with both victims and abusers. Key issues are:

o **assessment**

o **monitoring**

o **reviewing**

We cannot forget that we have to work with abusers as well. It is very natural that in some cases the worker may feel real dislike or even hatred towards the abuser, because of what s/he has done to the victim. These feelings have to be well hidden from the client. It is very important to try to understand why a person has abused a victim. There may well be ways of helping the abuser to comes to terms with what has happened and to work on any problems so that it is does not happen again. Workers will probably have more sympathy towards and be willing to work with a carer who has physically abused a dependent person because of the stress s/he is under rather than with the son who has raped his mother.

In Chapter 2 it was pointed out that there can be many reasons why an abusive situation can occur and work should not just focus on the problems of the victim. It is the aim of this chapter to consider how home care, residential and day care staff can help both victims and abusers in the long term.

Workers must come to terms with the fact that working with abuse can be a lengthy process. Victims may be very reluctant to disclose about what is happening to them and even when they do it can take years rather than months to help them through the healing process. Even if the abuse stops, the pain, hurt and trauma does not go away instantly.

So this is what the overall aim is in the long term, but what happens in between? Attention needs to be given to how work should be undertaken with both the victim and abuser after the initial investigation. It was mentioned in the previous chapter that if a person is at risk of abuse, a protection plan should be developed. A protection plan is a way of stating how workers are going to try to protect a victim of abuse. Some guidelines refer to such plans as actions plans, care plans etc. No matter what term is used, the plan should be seen as something separate from a care plan which might be part of the Community Care package. This plan is to **protect**, not just to care. Each protection plan needs to be clear by:

- **setting aims and objectives**

- **naming the workers involved**

- **stating the roles and tasks of each worker**

- **explaining if specific monitoring tools are to be used**

- **setting a date for review**

(1) Setting aims and objectives

The protection plan needs to spell out what exactly the plan is trying to achieve. General aims like 'to protect Mrs J' or 'to help Mr T' are not explicit enough.

(2) Naming the workers involved

A **keyworker** should be named (this is normally the social worker), in order to co-ordinate future work and ensure that the protection plan is implemented.

If someone sees the victim more frequently than the keyworker, then s/he should be named as the **primary worker** (for example this could be the home help, day centre worker).

Everyone else who is involved should be listed in the plan.

(3) Stating the roles and tasks of each worker

It is not good enough to say 'social worker will visit regularly'. What does regularly mean? To some workers it may be once a week; to others it may be once a month. Precise details are required. For example:

- Mrs Garton, social worker will visit on a twice weekly basis and will carry out a full needs assessment.

- District nurse visits on a daily basis to give insulin injection.

- Anne, care assistant, will be involved in reminiscence work with Mrs X twice a week (half hour sessions)

(4) Specific monitoring tools to be used

If specific tools/protocols are going to be used they should be written down in the protection plan. For example, home helps and day centre staff may agree to use bodycharts because a client is often presenting with injuries.

(5) Setting date for review

Abuse cases must not be left to drift. A definite date must be set for review. If there are serious concerns the case conference should be reconvened quite quickly in order to review the situation. Otherwise, cases are usually reviewed every three and six months.

At the end of this chapter are some examples of protection plans which have been used (see Protection Plans 1, 2 and 3).

*   *   *   *   *

This is all fine in theory, but what can home care and residential do in a practical sense? All workers need to know that they have something to contribute. How many times have we heard comments like:

- I'm only the home help
- I'm just a residential worker
- I've no real skills
- I'm not a professional
- I'm no-one important

It was said at the beginning of this chapter that working with abuse can be a lengthy process. This can be because the victim may choose to stay in the abusive situation and denies that s/he is being abused or because even if the abuse stops the victim needs to heal. Even with proper therapy this can sometimes take years.

Counselling victims is a very skilled job and it is certainly not the job of home care and residential staff to undertake this task. Even experienced social workers may not have all the skills to help or treat a victim of elder abuse. This is why sometimes specialized counsellors are brought in to work with victims (and abusers) using money from Community Care budgets. This also happens because many social workers just do not have the time to do thorough counselling over a long period of time.

Home care and residential/day care staff need to be aware of how victims can be healed, that is by addressing certain issues. This is important because the victim may start talking about certain things and workers need to know if they need to encourage the victim to talk about certain topics. It is also important to let the victim know it is all right to talk to the worker and it is all right to feel certain emotions. Victims need to talk about:

o **what has happened to them**

o **the actual abuse**

o **the abuser**

o **why they think it happened**

o **their true feelings**

o **the grief/loss**

o **letting go/moving on**

o **the future**

In the same way, abusers have to talk about the same issues but also they have to try to talk about:

o **why s/he abused the victim**

o **how s/he feels about the victim**

o **how s/he feels about having committed abuse**

It is important that workers use all the skills and techniques which were mentioned in Chapter 4 when discussing handling disclosure. The role in the long term role for home care and residential/day care staff is a supportive one, where they can listen and empathize with either the victim or the abuser and help them to move on to a better and safer future.

Suggested Reading

As nothing specific has been written on counselling older people who have been victims of elder abuse, I think it is useful to read around the subject of survivors. There is a lot of useful literature on working with adults who were sexually abused as children, but also about counselling women who have been victims of domestic violence. Much of the knowledge and techniques can be transferred to working with older people who have been victims of abuse.

Bass, E. and Davis, L. (1988) *The Courage to Heal*. New York: Harper and Row.

Burke Drauker, C. (1992) *Counselling Survivors of Childhood Sexual Abuse*. London: Sage.

Hoff, L.A. (1990) *Battered Women as Survivors*. London: Routledge.

Kenney, C. (1989) *Counselling the Survivors of Sexual Abuse*. Norwich: Social Work Monographs.

Sanderson, C. (1995) *Counselling Adult Survivors of Child Sexual Abuse*, 2nd edition. London: Jessica Kingsley.

✓

Protection Plan 1

Subject: Michael Greenburg

Background information

> Michael is a Jewish man aged 72, who has been abused financially by his neighbours over a number of years, but also by complete strangers who have befriended him for short periods of time. He has been very isolated for a number of years and has neglected himself.

Aims/Objectives

- To prevent Michael being abused financially in the future.
- To help Michael manage his money.
- To encourage Michael to socialize in a safe environment.

Keyworker: Social worker

Primary worker: Home help

Tasks/responsibilities

(1) Home care staff

- (a)   cash pension/pay bills
- (b)   open post office account – deposit surplus money after paying bills, shopping etc
- (c)   weekly shopping
- (d)   cleaning
- (e)   make one hot meal a day; encourage good nutrition; use kosher food
- (f)   take Michael shopping for new clothes

(2) District nurse

- (a)   dress leg ulcers; three times a week

(3) Social worker

- (a)   apply for place at day centre

(4) Rabbi

- (a)   to arrange for a volunteer to take Michael to the synagogue each Saturday

Review

3 months' time

✓

Subject: Gabriella Morton

Background information

> Mrs Morton has been physically abused by her daughter. This has been going on for sometime. Mrs Morton told the home help about the abuse and said that she had had enough. An elder abuse investigation has taken place. At her own request, Mrs Morton was removed to a temporary bed in a residential unit and has made a statement to the police. She wants to move into residential care on a permanent basis.

Aims/objectives

- To protect Mrs Morton from further abuse by her daughter
- To keep Mrs Morton in a safe environment
- To provide counselling for Mrs Morton

People involved

> Social worker (keyworker)
> Home help
> Residential staff (primary worker: Eleanor Wragg, care assistant)
> Police

Agreed work

> **Social worker** – over the next few weeks a full needs assessment will be carried out. Some counselling needs to be undertaken regarding the physical violence Mrs Morton has experienced, but also to ascertain whether Mrs Morton really does want permanent care or whether this is her initial reaction to the crisis.

> **Home help** – will visit Mrs Morton whilst she is in temporary care to maintain contact.

> **Residential staff** – will support Mrs Morton and contribute to the full needs assessment. Eleanor Wragg, care assistant, will be the primary worker for Mrs Morton, whilst in the unit. Staff will ensure that Mrs Morton's daughter does not have access to her mother.

> **Police** – will proceed with their investigation

> **Mrs Morton** – will remain in the temporary bed for the next month

Case Conference

> To be reconvened in one month.

✓

Subject: Bertha Hart

Main aim

> To prevent Bertha being sexually abused by her son in the future.

Background information

> Bertha, who suffers from Alzheimers Disease, was sexually abused by her son, Terence, two years ago. He was sent to prison but is now due to be released. Terence is known to be very violent. Bertha is now a permanent resident in an old people's home. A case conference was convened to discuss her future protection.

Roles:

> **Probation officer** – informed the case conference that Terence wishes to visit his mother regularly. Probation officer will discuss the decisions of the case conference with Terence and go through the protection plan with him. The probation officer has the responsibility to support Terence and see him regularly.

> **Residential staff** – will ensure that all visits from Terence are supervised and carried out in public areas, so that Bertha and staff are not put at any risk. They will monitor and keep a written record of the visits (noting Bertha's reactions, behaviour etc).

> **Social worker** – will be the keyworker to co-ordinate the implementation of the protection plan

Decisions

> Because Bertha has repeatedly said that she wants to see Terence, it will be suggested to him that he visits her on a fortnightly basis until the case conference is reconvened in two months' time. If residential staff have any concerns about the situation, the case conference will be convened at an earlier date.

8 Residential/Day Care I
The Theory

Abuse in institutions is a very much neglected area. People have known for years that abuse does happen, but it has often been swept under the carpet. A problem is that often the victims of this type of abuse are extremely vulnerable and unable to speak out for fear of retribution. Also, who is going to believe them?

The purpose of this chapter is consider the forms of abuse which may take place in institutions and why abuse may be occurring. The following chapter is more practical in that it helps the reader to concentrate on how to identify abuse and how to work with cases of abuse.

WHAT IS AN INSTITUTION?

The Oxford English Dictionary defines 'institution' as:

> establishment in cure of souls; established law, custom or practice

When I use the word institution in this text I am referring to hospitals, day centres local authority homes and homes in the private sector. Participants have often got annoyed with me on courses because I use the word institution:

> 'I work in a home, not an institution'

> 'It is a place where people live. It is not an institution, it's people's home'

Although we are trying to ensure that people feel it is their home, realistically it cannot be like home in the community. There are certain forces in place which make any 'home', however well run, an institution. There have to be rules and regulations to run the home and sometimes regimes come into existence. Cultures which exist within a home can be abusive themselves, but we shall return to that point later.

WHAT IS ABUSE IN AN INSTITUTION?

All the types of abuse, that is the five categories of abuse mentioned in Chapter 1, can occur in an institution. Particular areas which workers need to focus on are abusive practices and attitudes. Very little work has been done in this area, but the

London Borough of Enfield Social Services Department has defined institutional abuse in its guidelines since 1988 and other authorities have tended to adopt both the definitions and the indicators, which are shown in Handouts 8.1 and 8.2.

WHO ABUSES?

It is very important for everyone to remember that there can be many 'types' of abusers. Whenever you talk about abuse in institutions people immediately think about staff abusing residents. This does happen, but abuse which occurs in institutions can be much more complex and this needs to be addressed in training sessions concerned with institutional abuse. Handout 8.3 can be used as a basis for discussion with workers.

A Member of Staff can Abuse a Resident

Perhaps the most common scenario is one of physical abuse. Staff may become very tired and frustrated with a resident who is heavily dependent and s/he may lash out in a fit of temper.

CASE EXAMPLE

Annabel worked as a night care assistant to get some extra money. Her husband was badly paid and they had three children under five, including a six-month-old baby, who did not sleep very much. Annabel was often extremely tired when she came on duty and many of the residents were highly dependent. Annabel lost her temper on several occasions and one day she held a pillow over a female resident's face.

We are also aware that sometimes people choose to work in institutions because they know the residents are extremely vulnerable and easy targets. A worrying fact is that often police checks are not carried out on staff, who may move frequently between establishments in both local authorities and the private sector.

CASE EXAMPLE

Morgan sexually abused two older women in a private nursing home. The matron reported it to the inspection unit. The inspection officer checked where he had worked before. He had worked in two other nursing homes where he had done the same thing but the owners had not reported it and just sacked him. Morgan did have a criminal record but police checks had never been done.

A Resident can Abuse a Member of Staff

Many staff are repeatedly abused by their residents and I get very annoyed when they tell me that their managers have said 'That is your job. Get on with it'.

CASE EXAMPLES

Marlene came to dread keyworker sessions with Ted, because he always wanted to talk about sexual matters, which embarrassed Marlene. On several occasions he touched her breasts.

Rose was dementing. She constantly swore at staff and threw things at them. One day she hit a care assistant with a vase. The care assistant ended up in hospital with concussion.

No staff member should be a victim of abuse and work needs to be done with all staff groups about what constitutes abuse towards them. I find many staff accept abusive behaviour because they believe the resident 'cannot help it' or 'you cannot do anything about it' or 'it doesn't really matter. It only happens occasionally'. If a resident is abusive, then an investigation should be carried out and the situation dealt with because no staff member should be put at risk.

A Resident can Abuse another Resident

Once again these situations have to be dealt with and cannot be ignored for the same reasons as above. Residents, like staff, should not be put at risk.

CASE EXAMPLES

Ron was perfectly mentally sound. He liked to spend time with Clara, who was severely demented and who had been sexually abused by her son previously. Ron started fondling Clara's breasts in public areas which was commented upon by other residents to staff. No action was taken until a member of staff found him with his hand in Clara's knickers, whilst she was pinned up against a corridor wall.

Residents on one landing did not like Leroy because he was black. They called him 'nigger' and 'black bastard' to his face and told him to get out of their lounge.

An Outsider can Abuse a Resident

People are often under the misconception that once a resident is placed permanently in a home s/he is safe. However, there are many opportunities where an outsider can come in and abuse a resident.

✝✝ Madge has Alzheimer's Disease and was sexually abused by her son, Tom. The social worker never shared this information with the residential staff when Madge was placed in the unit. Two years later Tom started to visit. He said he had just come back to live in the area after working abroad. In fact he had just been released from prison. Whenever, Tom visited his mother he always insisted that he 'wanted some privacy' and insisted on seeing his mother in her bedroom. He continued to sexually abuse her.

✝✝ Amy had worked as a volunteer for many years for different agencies. She then became interested in a local advocacy scheme and visited several residents in Elmwood Grove. Eventually, staff found out that she was taking money from residents.

WHY DOES ABUSE HAPPEN IN INSTITUTIONS?

There is not usually just one straightforward reason why abuse happens in an institution; it can be a culmination of reasons. The most common ones are summarized in Handout 8.4.

Lack of Education/Training

In this country we are very bad at educating children and young people about older people. Consequently, many youngsters have ageist attitudes and in fact our society generally tends to be very ageist. There is a lack of awareness about the ageing process and what can happen to an older person in later life. The positives aspects are conveniently forgotten as well. In America and Canada education programmes include awareness programmes about older people. Programmes 'positively influence children's attitudes towards ageing and older people and are designed to use with children as young as four years old (The Ontario Network for the Prevention of Elder Abuse 1991).

Some people come to work in a residential unit because they *need* a job, not because they *want* to do the job. They may have no idea about how to work with older people and may come with all sorts of ageist attitudes. A common trend at the moment seems to be for young people, who leave school and cannot claim income support, to go and work for very low wages in the private sector. They receive little or no training.

In other situations workers are not given training on a regular basis or it is not appropriate training. Established staff who have been there for years 'know it all' because they 'have been on care for years' and you 'can't teach me anything', so they refuse to go on any training.

CASE EXAMPLE

Edna had worked in Burston Heath for ten years. She never gave time to let residents try and dress themselves. She liked to 'get on and get the job done', because she considered herself to be a 'fast worker'.

Staff Groups/Factions

Sometimes members of staff form into groups of 'friends' and factions exist between these groups. One group of workers may see themselves as having power either because they have been there longer or because they just think they are better. If such factions exist it can have a detrimental effect on both staff and residents.

CASE EXAMPLE

One group of staff insist on having their coffee break first. If a resident comes to the workers when they are having their break, they tell the resident to 'go away'.

The Manager

There can be two types of manager – the strong one and the weak one. The strong one may be a very good manager who does the job efficiently and professionally. Alternatively, the strong manager who abuses his/her position runs a tight regime, where maybe neither staff nor residents are listened to and hence abusive situations can occur. The weak manager does not manage the unit – perhaps the strong factions of staff run the unit how they like or think it should be run.

CASE EXAMPLES

Some of the staff group want to organize a jumble sale to raise funds to buy a video for the residents, who would like to rent their favourite films from the local video shop. The manager says the residents do not 'need' a video when televisions are available.

In one unit, a principal has been persuaded to let two members of staff take responsibility for the duty rotas. These two workers make sure they and their friends get the off duty and holidays they want before the other members of staff are asked.

Existing Regimes

It has been said already that institutions have to have some rules and regulations, but sometimes strict regimes can abuse both the staff and residents.

CASE EXAMPLE

Meals are at set times to suit the hours the cook works.

The Environment

The physical environment can be totally depressing both for the staff and for the residents. Some buildings are just not suited to be 'a home'. An example is when a building is like a rabbit warren and residents find it difficult to find their way around. Things like furnishings are important. If the walls are drab, then residents and staff alike may become totally depressed if they have to live and work in this atmosphere.

CASE EXAMPLE

Residents are not allowed to decorate their rooms in bright colours. They are told their chosen colours must blend in with the rest of the home whose basic colours are brown and cream.

Low Staff Morale

Low morale can be caused by a number of reasons. Staff may feel undervalued by managers and by residents. Nobody ever tells them that they are doing a good job. Nowadays in local authority homes staff feel frustrated because of low staffing levels. Often they would like to do more imaginative work with residents, but most of the time all they are doing is giving basic care. They cannot spend enough time with residents on a one-to-one basis or even do groupwork. Workers feel that some managers check up on them if they spend 'too much time talking to residents'.

CASE EXAMPLE

Care assistant said 'I feel like I am serving time with the residents. Just waiting for them to die. There is no quality of life for them and no job satisfaction for me'.

The Characteristics of the Staff

Some people are just not suited to working with older people or within the residential sector because of their own characteristics/personality. Indeed they may have particular problems which should impede them from working with older people, for example, a history of sex offending.

CASE EXAMPLE

Terry was a kleptomaniac. He had been fined several times for shoplifting. He always got jobs working in private rest homes where he stole money and possessions from residents.

Characteristics of Residents

If the dependency levels are very high in a unit, the workers may get very tired and frustrated, especially if staffing levels are low. They may feel that they are not achieving anything positive.

CASE EXAMPLE

All the residents in Manor House were demented and doubly incontinent. Care staff spent their days toiletting, feeding and changing the residents. The 'worst' residents were kept together in one room and left 'to get on with it'. They received no stimulation at all.

A CODE OF PRACTICE

All managers and staff should consider what is an acceptable code of good practice in their unit. It is no use saying everything is fine and 'our home is lovely'. No home is perfect and improvements can always be made. Workers need to be honest about what is going on by focussing on **attitudes** and **practices**. Work should be done to consider what is wrong in the unit at the present time and how attitudes and practices could be improved. In the following chapter Exercise 9.6 will focus on developing such a code of good practice, by considering the values which should exist in a residential setting (Social Services Inspectorate 1989).

SUGGESTED READING

S. Biggs, C. Phillipson and P. Kingston (eds) (1995) 'Institutional care and elder mistreatment.' In *Elder Abuse in Perspective*. Buckingham: Open University Press, Chapter 6.

Gilleard, C. (1994) 'Physical abuse in homes and hospitals.' In M. Eastman (ed) *Old Age Abuse: A New Perspective*. London: Chapman and Hall, Chapter 7.

London Borough of Enfield (1993) *Notes of Guidance (Practice and Procedure). Abuse of Vulnerable Adults*, section 5.

Social Services Inspectorate (1989) *Homes are for Living in.* London: HMSO.

The Ontario Network for the Prevention of Elder Abuse (1991) *Old Friends: A Storytelling Kit About Old Age.* Toronto: The Ontario Network for the Prevention of Elder Abuse.

Institutional Abuse

(1) There is individual abuse, where a resident or residents are hit, are verbally abused or have their money stolen or misused.

(2) The regime of the establishment regiments the residents:

(a) residents awakened too early in the morning

(b) lack of flexibility in choice in the time of going to bed

(c) lack of opportunity for getting drinks and snacks

(d) lack of choice and consultation about meals; the last meal being served too early

(e) lack of personal possessions, furniture, telephone, TV, radio etc

(f) lack of procedure for washing, mending and marking personal clothing

(g) lack of toiletting facilities

(h) clothing dirty and unkempt, often with no underwear

(i) poor handling of medical complaints.

FROM: London Borough of Enfield (1993) *Notes of Guidance (Practice and Procedure) Abuse of Vulnerable Adults.*

Possible Signs of Institutional Abuse

(1) Institutional abuse (that can lead to individual abuse):

(a) Failure to agree within the managing agency about the purpose or/and tasks of the home

(b) Failure to manage life in the centre/home in an appropriate way. (When things go wrong they are not sorted out, e.g. maintenance of building)

(c) Poor standards of cleanliness

(d) Low staffing levels over a long period of time

(e) Lack of knowledge or confusion about guidelines

(f) Breakdown of communication between managers of the home

(g) Staff factions (result often of 'f')

(h) Staff working the hours to suit them

(i) Staff may drink heavily on and off duty

(j) Staff ordering residents around or even shouting at them

(k) Lack of positive communication with residents

(l) Low staff morale

(m) Failure by management to see a *pattern* of events which often are treated as individual instances in isolation

(n) Punitive methods adopted by staff against residents

FROM: London Borough of Enfield (1993) *Notes of Guidance (Practice and Procedure) Abuse of Vulnerable Adults*

Institutional Abuse
Victims and Abusers

You must remember that different people can be
victims and abusers, for example:

- A member of staff can abuse a resident

- A resident can abuse a member of staff

- A resident can abuse another resident

- An outsider can abuse a resident

Root Causes of Abuse in Institutions

- Lack of education/training

- Staff groups/factions

- The manager

- Existing regimes

- The environment

- Low staff morale

- Low staffing levels

- The characteristics of the staff

- The characteristics of the residents

9 Residential/Day Care 2
The Exercises

This chapter includes many different exercises that can be used to train residential and day care workers. Trainers should use the material in conjunction with earlier chapters to develop issues which have been raised. Some of the exercises are extensions of earlier ones, but are designed specifically for residential and day care staff.

ABUSE IN INSTITUTIONS

Exercise 9.1 is to move workers on to think about what types of abuse can happen in institutions. When I use the word institution I am referring to hospitals, day centres, local authority homes and homes in the private sector.

* * * * *

Handout 9.1(a) can be used for a large group discussion or exercise.

RESPONDING TO SITUATIONS

Residential and day care staff may be the people to hear disclosure about abuse, because a victim has come to trust them. A victim may blurt something out when it is least expected; usually when doing something of a personal/intimate nature. No-one can ever be fully prepared for this, so it is important that workers think about what could be said to them if a client reveals that s/he is being abused or perhaps if an abuser admits to having done something. Exercises 9.2 and 9.3 will help workers to think about how they would react in these situations and more crucially what they would actually say to the victim.

PROFESSIONAL DILEMMAS

The concept of the professional dilemma has been discussed in detail elsewhere (Riley 1989; Pritchard 1995, p.19). Exercise 9.4 presents dilemmas which residential and day care staff may face.

HANDLING ABUSE SITUATIONS

It is important that workers spend time thinking about what they would actually do in certain situations and the previous exercises will help them to do this. However, it is not enough just to think about what should be done immediately and in the short term. Abusive situations can be ongoing because behaviours are repetitive. Workers in residential settings must contemplate how they can prevent abuse reoccurring. Exercise 9.5 is designed so that workers will think about their immediate reactions, but also they are required to think about the long term.

GOOD PRACTICE

Everyone who works in a residential unit or in a day centre, no matter what their job is, must consider what is good practice. A way to do this effectively and to develop good practices for the future is to get staff to develop a code of good practice for their place of work. Exercise 9.6 helps groups of staff work together to achieve this.

SUGGESTED READING

Pritchard, J. (1995) *The Abuse of Older People*, 2nd edition. London: Jessica Kingsley.

Riley, P. (1989) *Professional Dilemmas in Elder Abuse*, (unpublished).

Social Services Inspectorate (1989) *Homes are for living in*. London HMSO.

ABUSE OR NOT ABUSE?

Objective

To make participants think about what constitutes abuse in institutional settings

Participants

Exercise to be carried out in small groups

Equipment

Prepare photocopies of handout(s) with situations to be considered

Time

Groups spend 3 minutes on each situation (30 minutes in total).

Task

Each group will consider and discuss the scenarios on the handout. It is the task of the group to reach a consensus of opinion about whether this is a case of abuse or not. If the group agrees it is abuse, they must decide which category (or categories) of abuse, i.e. physical, emotional, financial, neglect, sexual, the case fits in to.

Feedback

The trainer takes feedback by going through each scenario and finding out what each group's consensus was; s/he also asks whether there were areas of disagreement in the groups.

Abuse or Not Abuse?

Ella is suffering from dementia. She picks up food from another resident's plate and eats it with her fingers. The care assistant slaps Ella's hand when she sees her do this.

Elizabeth is very frail but she likes to wander with her zimmer frame and on a couple of occasions she has been found outside. When she does wander about she tends to fall. Staff now regularly sit her in a chair in front of the television and they place a tray across the chair so that she cannot get out.

Care assistant says to Cyril 'I bet you were a right one when you were younger. How many times could you get it up in one night?'

Walter is slightly incontinent and tends to have some accidents during the daytime. He is now made to sit everyday in a chair by his bed without any trousers on and a blanket is put over his knees.

Lily has been taken to the toilet and left there. The care assistant said she would come back in a few minutes. Lily is still sitting there ten minutes later.

Richard is a 70-year-old man, who is deaf and has learning difficulties. He is not allowed to play dominoes with other day centre users, because the staff say he 'messes' up the game because he cannot hear the other players knock their dominoes.

Melanie suffers from schizophrenia. When she attends day centre, one worker always says to her '*Who* are we today then?'

Betty has regular respite care in Silver Birch House. She has complained to female staff that Eric, a male care assistant, always touches her bottom when he is standing talking to her. The female staff have said 'He does that to all of us, so what?'

Anthony has many physical disabilities. He has difficulty eating, but can manage by himself. However, he takes a lot of time to finish meals and makes a mess everywhere. In a unit where he has respite care and attends day centre, he is made to wear a bib at mealtimes and some members of staff call him 'Baby Tony'.

A day centre worker refuses to include Mary in a group Christmas shopping trip, because she says she 'smells and would be an embarrassment in public'.

WHAT WOULD YOU SAY IF...?

Objective

To make participants think about what they would say if they found themselves in a certain situation.

Participants

Exercise to be carried out in small groups

Equipment

Handouts to be photocopied beforehand

Flipchart paper and pens

Time

5 minutes to complete each scenario

Task

Participants are asked to consider and discuss in their groups each scenario in turn and write down the actual *words/sentences* they would *say* if they found themselves in that situation.

What Would You Say?

- A confused resident says that a male resident slept in her bed last night.

- Bridget, who is Irish, says she hates living in the home because other residents are always making fun of her and telling Irish jokes in front of her.

- You walk into the entrance hall and find a district nurse dressing a resident's leg ulcers.

- Your new principal says that all residents must be up and dressed by 9.00 a.m.

- Robert, who has come in for a short term stay, says he never wants to go home because his wife 'batters' him.

- A nephew brings his uncle in for his first respite stay. He asks you to make sure that his uncle is tied into his wheelchair to stop him falling out, because that is how they cope with him at home.

- You overhear a colleague talking about an Afro-Caribbean resident to another care assistant: 'That black bastard shouldn't be taking up one of our beds'.

- You are bathing Maria when you see lacerations all down her back.

- A colleague tells you that s/he has slapped a client across the face.

- Eleanor says she is 'frightened' of her daughter.

- A man who comes to day centre says that local teenagers are coming into his house and taking money from him.

- You walk into the lounge and see George spit on his wife.

WHAT WOULD YOU DO IF?

Objective

To make participants think about how they would react and what action they would take if they found themselves in certain situations

Participants

Exercise to be carried in pairs

Equipment

Situations to be written out on cards by the trainer beforehand (taken from handout)

Pen and paper

Time

15 minutes to discuss two scenarios

Task

Each participant is given a card and asked to consider the situation with their partner. Each pair must write down what actions they would take.

© Jacki Pritchard, 1996

Some Possible Situations for Cards

You see a male care assistant pat a female resident on the bottom.

A colleague is always rushing one particular client and regularly transports her by wheelchair rather than letting her try to walk.

Jemima openly talks about the fact that she is a lesbian. Today you hear her shouting for help and when you get into her room you find a male resident lying on top of her.

You see a colleague give a confused Jewish man an ordinary meal. When you remind her that he always has a kosher meal prepared for him, she says she cannot be bothered to fetch it.

You hear day centre users making fun of a Somalian man, because his English is not very good.

When John comes to the day centre today, he tells you that his son has hit his demented wife with her walking stick.

Last week a service user was found masturbating in the toilet. This week your colleague keeps referring to him as a 'pervert'.

A service user confides in you that her son forces her to watch pornographic videos with him. She does not like it.

PROFESSIONAL DILEMMAS

Objective

To make participants consider what they would do if faced with a dilemma.

Participants

This exercise is to be carried out in pairs

Equipment

Instruction sheet and cards to be prepared beforehand.

Pen and paper

Time

Each pair is given a card to consider and discuss for 15 minutes.

Task

Participants have to consider the dilemma on the card and discuss whether they *would* take some action or whether they would leave the situation as it is. They have to write down their reasons for *doing* or *not doing*.

Feedback

The trainer should ask:

- Whether most participants agreed with their partner?
- If there were any areas of disagreement what were they?
- Do participants want to raise any issues or ask about things they were unsure about.

Instruction Sheet

Definition of a professional dilemma

A professional dilemma is a situation in which a person who has a specialist knowledge is confronted by choices between equally unacceptable alternatives. It is about **doing** and sometimes about **not doing**.

Task

1. Read the situation described on the card which has been given to you.

2. Consider what you would *do* or *not do*.

3. Write down your reasons for *doing* or *not doing*.

Some Professional Dilemmas

Lily has come in for a short term stay. You are helping her to bath when you notice bruises on her arms, legs and buttocks. When you ask Lily how she got the bruises, she said she cannot remember. Lucy is perfectly mentally sound.

Beryl keeps telling you that she is frightened of her keyworker, Sam, but she will not say why. Today, you see Sam standing outside Beryl's room. He seems to be pulling up his trousers and zipping his fly.

Frank comes in for regular respite care. He lives with his 24-year-old granddaughter, who has children aged 4, 2 and 3 months. When Frank is admitted for his latest stay he is badly bruised around the face. His granddaughter is with him when you ask about his face. She says Frank fell out of his wheelchair. Frank says that is a lie and that his granddaughter hit him.

You are absolutely convinced that one of your colleagues, Anita, is giving some residents too much medication. You also suspect that she drinks whilst on duty. You decide to tell your principal about this. When you report your suspicions, the principal refuses to take any action and tells you 'not to be so imaginative' and that 'Anita is an excellent worker, who is one in a million'.

You and Tracey work in the day centre. Some of the users have confided in you that they have been buying things from Tracey's catalogue and paying her a bit of money each week. Now they have received notices from the catalogue company saying no payments have been received. The users are very worried but 'don't want to get Tracey into trouble'.

You are a day centre worker. Today you walk into the toilets and see that one of the users is hitting another user and calling her 'a silly old cow'.

Lucy has not attended day centre for eight weeks. The day centre staff have started to visit Lucy at home. On the last visit, your colleague noticed that Lucy had a black eye and a bruise on her neck. Today you see that she has a cut lip. Lucy says that she keeps going dizzy and falling over. The social worker has told you that the GP says Lucy is fit and healthy. Lucy lives with her son, who is unemployed.

Annie has been coming to day centre for the past 10 years. She has always talked about the violence she has suffered from her husband and son. She does not want anyone to do anything except listen to her. Today she arrives at day centre and shows you that her right arm is covered in cigarette burns. Again she refuses to take any action, including going to hospital.

When Sydney first started attending day centre six months ago he was the life and soul of the centre and wanted to be involved in everything. He made a lot of new friends and really enjoyed himself. However, you have noticed a change in Sydney during the past six weeks. He has become very thin, he wants to sit by himself and rarely talks to anyone. He says nothing is wrong when you find him crying.

Ellen is 65 years old and has learning disabilities. She is deaf and cannot speak. When you walk into the kitchen you see another day centre worker holding Ellen's hand under the hot water tap. When you confront the worker, she says Ellen put her hand under the tap and she was trying to pull it away.

© Jacki Pritchard, 1996

HANDLING ABUSE

Objective

To make participants think about how they would handle abusive situations both in the short term and the long term.

Participants

To work in small groups

Equipment

Flipchart paper and pens

Time

10 minutes to be spent on each scenario

Task

Participants are asked to consider an abusive situation in their group. The group is to discuss and answer three questions:

- **What would you do there and then?**

- **What would you say to the people involved?**

- **What would you do in the future to stop this happening again?**

Abusive Situations

Staff member abuses resident

A care assistant tells a resident she cannot come out of her room, because she has been naughty.

Sharon is a domestic and when she is working on the corridor she insists on playing Radio 1 very loudly on the radio. The residents complain but she ignores them.

Cook tells Eric he cannot have a pudding because he has not eaten his vegetables.

When the Deputy is on nights, she says all the residents have to be in bed by 10.00p.m.

Resident abuses a member of staff

Cornelius can get agitated if he has to wait for anything. Today he hits you with his stick on your arm to get your attention.

A resident deliberately urinates on a care assistant when she is trying to find his slippers under the bed.

Two male residents always sit together and continuously make sexual remarks to female staff.

When you are bathing Clarence, he touches your breasts as you are leaning over the bath.

© Jacki Pritchard, 1996

Resident abuses resident

A group of female residents tell Eliza that she cannot sit in their lounge because she 'does not fit in' and she's 'not one of us'. Eliza is Afro-Caribbean.

Theo openly brags about his sexual conquests past and present. Today you find him having sexual intercourse with Josephine, who is severely demented.

Basil makes fun of Millie because she needs help getting in and out of her wheelchair.

A resident swears at one particular resident every time he sees him.

Outsiders abuse residents

Mrs Agneau says her mother cannot go on the summer trip to Blackpool, because she will get too tired and it will cost money.

You hear a volunteer say to a resident 'You must give me some money for visiting you'.

You see Mr Carruthers putting his penis into his sister Lottie's mouth. Lottie suffers from dementia and thinks most men are her husband.

Glen visits his grandmother once a month. He always promises to visit next week, but never does. His grandmother gets very upset when he does not appear the following week.

DEVELOPING A CODE OF GOOD PRACTICE

Objective

To get workers to focus on attitudes and practices which exist in their unit at the present time and to develop a code of good practice for future use in the unit

Participants

To work in staff groups

Equipment

Handouts 9.6a, b, and c and pens

Time

30 minutes

Task

To have a staff group discussion about what is good and bad about the unit as it is now. Then to further the discussion by answering the questions on the sheet.

A Code of Good Practice

In order to develop a code of good practice, you need to focus on the

- ○ **values**

- ○ **current practices and attitudes**

- ○ **expectations of staff, residents and managers**

You can do this by considering the list of values (see Handout 9.6b) and answering the following questions:

(1) Do these values exist in your unit?

(2) In what ways could they be improved?

(3) Are there any problems with current practices?

(4) Are there are any problems with currents attitudes (consider those of both staff and residents)

(5) What should residents expect from staff?

(6) What should staff expect from residents?

(7) What should staff expect from managers?

(8) What should managers expect from staff?

The Values

Privacy

The right of individuals to be left alone or undisturbed and free from intrusion or public attention into their affairs

Dignity

Recognition of the intrinsic value of people regardless of circumstances by respecting their uniqueness and their personal needs; treating with respect

Independence

Opportunities to act and think without reference to another person, including a willingness to incur a degree of calculated risk

Choice

Opportunity to select independently from a range of options

Rights

The maintenance of all entitlements associated with citizenship

Fulfilment

The realization of personal aspirations and abilities in all aspects of daily life

FROM: Social Services Inspectorate (1989) *Homes are for living in*. London HMSO

A Code of Good Practice

FOR

....

(Name of unit)

We should be achieving a code of good practice by

Abuse of Not Abuse?

- A resident is not allowed to have a hot water bottle in his bed because the Principal considers it to be a health and safety risk.

- A Polish woman is placed in a home where no-one can speak Polish.

- Meals are served at set times. If a resident does not want to eat at the 'normal' time, they can have a sandwich later.

- Every time a day centre worker talks to Alice she mimics her Welsh accent.

- Jasper's fluid intake is restricted because he is incontinent.

- Staff always serve hot drinks from large jugs with milk and sugar in because it saves time.

- A care assistant has called a resident 'a dirty git' ever since she found him masturbating in the bathroom.

- An Asian man is given meat to eat. It is not considered to be important to follow his religious beliefs because he is confused.

- A worker throws cold water over a resident when bathing him because he starts talking about sexual matters.

- A Day Centre Manager screams at a worker that she is 'useless' in front of the service users.

- A thirteen-year-old boy always takes £2 from his grandma's purse when he visits. He promises to buy her flowers because she misses her garden. He never brings her flowers.

- Staff organize a make-up party one evening. The female residents are not invited.

- Day centre staff decide that they would like to go to Scarborough for the summer day trip out. Users are not asked where they would like to go.

- Residents are not allowed to have their own face cloths. They have to use the ones the care assistants carry in their overall pockets.

- Incontinent day centre users are made to sit in chairs nearest the toilet.

10 Issues for Managers

It is not just social work managers who have a responsibility to manage elder abuse cases. Home care organizers and senior staff in residential/day care settings also have responsibilities. This chapter will consider the key issues for these managers in working with cases of elder abuse.

MANAGERS AND ELDER ABUSE

Home care and residential/day care managers can face all sorts of problems in the area of elder abuse. One of their major roles is to manage staff who are working with elder abuse cases, so they need to know about what constitutes abuse, procedures, good practice and support. A manager can face a variety of problems, some of which are:

- a worker is abusing a client **unintentionally**
- a worker is abusing a client **deliberately**
- a worker fails to recognize an abusive situation
- a worker fails to acknowledge that his/her practice is abusive
- a worker does not **want** to work with abuse
- a worker **denies** that abuse is happening
- a worker breaks confidentiality and puts a client at risk
- a worker feels frustrated that a client wants to remain in the abusive situation
- a worker feels it is a waste of time trying to work with abuse cases because nothing can be done/there are no statutory powers
- cultures of mistreatment exist within a unit
- a resident is abusing other residents
- a resident is abusing staff

So managers have to develop ways of dealing with these problems and to develop coping strategies, because managing these difficulties can be very stressful.

SUPPORT FOR WORKERS

Working with elder abuse can be very frustrating and extremely stressful for any worker. It is very sad that some people still see working with older people as 'an easy option'. It is certainly not easy and working with elder abuse can be just as traumatic as working with child abuse. Even if workers are only on the periphery, elder abuse can raise all sorts of personal and professional issues for them, for example:

- they may see/hear things they have never thought about before e.g. the actual acts involved in sexual abuse
- it may remind them of their own personal experiences
- they may feel inadequate/a failure/ powerless.

Therefore, it is crucial that *all* managers develop efficient and effective ways of supporting workers who are involved with cases of elder abuse. This should begin with regular supervision sessions for all workers whether it is individual or group supervision. I know time is precious and other things may seem more important, but if workers cannot have individual supervision sessions, then group sessions should occur as often as possible.

However, some workers may need additional support, especially if they are involved in an elder abuse investigation. Managers must also be there for the worker when a situation is being monitored. The worker needs to feedback regularly about the situation and to discuss his/her role in working with the case. The manager has to be updated regularly in case a referral has to be made for an elder abuse investigation to take place.

Therefore a manager must:

- be accessible and ready to listen
- be able to give practical advice and emotional support
- give workers the opportunity to vent their feelings and anxieties

During an investigation, a worker may need to feedback regularly what is happening both to the client and to the worker. Sometimes if the worker has experienced abuse him/herself, in the past or currently, s/he may have the need to talk about it. In some cases it may be appropriate to suggest and then refer him/her on for specialist counselling if the manager cannot offer this personally. Some departments do employ specialist counsellors for their workers.

Elsewhere I have suggested some methods of supervision (Pritchard 1995, pp.85–98), which could be useful to help manage elder abuse cases more effectively. Other specific methods which could be employed to help all staff develop their skills in working with elder abuse are:

- discussion of specific issues/problems which crop up
- discussion of cases
- analysis of practice/what has happened
- role play in order to practice dealing with situations
- specific exercises designed to encourage the worker to vent his/her feelings
- use of videos/other training materials

All the above could be done in group supervision sessions or team development meetings (see below). All it takes is small amounts of time to undertake certain topics.

Case Examples

EXAMPLE 1 – HOME CARE

A home help, Margaret, is worried that her client, Eveleen, is being physically abused by her son, who is known to have served time in prison for violent crimes. Margaret has done a training course on working with elder abuse and knows she should be monitoring Eveleen's injuries. Eveleen is mentally sound and Margaret knows she must discuss the situation with her, but has put off doing so because she is 'really scared, because I know Eveleen will tell her son whatever I say to her'.

In a group supervision session, the home help's manager asked the other home helps how they would feel in this situation and what they would do. She did this by brainstorming with a flipchart, asking two questions:

'How would you feel in that situation?'

'What would you say to the client?'

Margaret felt very supported because other workers said they would be scared as well. She had thought that some of her colleagues would see her 'as being soft'. What also helped was that another home help talked about a similar case she had had when she worked in another area. This home help went into great detail about her own feelings, but also about the work she did to help the client talk about her real feelings towards the abuser. This gave Margaret something to focus on for her client and during the following week she plucked up courage to talk to Eveleen.

EXAMPLE 2 – RESIDENTIAL SETTING

In a staff meeting the principal of an old people's home wanted to discuss Mrs Elliot, who was going to visit the unit. Mrs Elliot had been sexually abused by a member of staff in a private rest home. Many of the staff expressed horror that such a thing could happen and this led to a full discussion about abuse in institutions. Some workers just could not believe that older people are abused in homes. The principal knew the Training Department had a video of a documentary which had been shown on television the year before, which included older people talking about the abuse they had experienced. The principal showed this video at the next staff meeting.

TEAM DEVELOPMENT MEETINGS

When I talk about team development meetings people always smile at me as though I am quite mad. They say they have no time. But as I said earlier in this book you have to *make* time if you are going to work successfully with elder abuse and promote good practice. Neither managers nor workers can just go on a training course and then 'do it'. You learn by doing, but along the way you have to face many problems and you make many mistakes. You and other people can learn by these mistakes and experiences.

Every worker must reflect on practice and share experiences (good and bad!). Perhaps we spend too much time considering the negatives. Good things do happen and there are success stories. We need to talk about these as well. Managers must not forget to value their workers and *tell* them when they have done well.

Team development meetings are a way of focussing on how to improve the way the team is functioning. Elder abuse can be taken as an area of work which needs to be developed. Team development meetings should happen regularly; ideally every three or six months. The team needs to:

- meet away from the worksite
- set objectives (what are you going to do with the time?)
- review (how are you working with elder abuse?)
- invite other people who you work with on cases of abuse (social workers, local police, district nurses) to help you and share problems

It is very necessary to plan what is going to happen in the team development meetings, that is, set some objectives about what you want to achieve, or else the meetings will drift and workers will moan that they are a waste of time. Some typical objectives which staff groups have set are:

- After six months all workers will be familiar with the departmental guidelines on elder abuse.
- We want to know more about identifying physical injuries. Must get an expert in – perhaps GP, consultant
- Staff feel they could abuse black elders because they know so little about different cultures. Have a session planning how we can learn more.
- Get social worker in to talk about what happens at a formal case conference.
- What are the boundaries of confidentiality in elder abuse cases? Let's discuss and get it clear for everyone.

TRAINING FOR MANAGERS

It is all very well for me to be writing about managers managing and supporting their staff who are working with elder abuse, but a manager cannot do this unless s/he has had the training. There is often this expectation that if you are a manager you know everything. This is not true at all. Therefore, it is important that home care managers and residential/day care managers let their training officers know what their training needs are in this area of work.

I am aware that in many authorities the grass roots workers are the first people to get the training on elder abuse. They then complain that they get no support from their managers because the managers have not had the training and do not know what the worker is talking about! Managers have to be honest that elder abuse is a new area of work and they *need* training in order to learn about the subject. I think it useful to have managers and workers training together for raising awareness and intervention skills, but then to have special sessions for managers to raise management issues.

MANAGERS NEED SUPPORT TOO

We must not forget that managers also need support both from their staff and from their peer groups and senior managers. It is important that managers form support networks for themselves. If senior managers are not supportive then first line managers must look to their peer group for support. In some departments managers meet regularly for support and then discuss the problems they are encountering (e.g. with certain parts of the guidelines; other agencies) in working with elder abuse. They then develop strategies to deal with the issues. Managers need to say how they are feeling too. They experience stress in the same ways as workers who are dealing with abuse and so they also need to develop support networks, so that they have somewhere to go to vent their feelings.

ALLEGATIONS OF ABUSE AGAINST STAFF

One of the greatest nightmares of any worker is being accused of something s/he has not done. This can happen especially where maybe a confused client makes allegations (e.g. saying the home care assistant has stolen money; accusing a residential worker of hitting a client). Many staff groups feel very vulnerable because allegations can be made against them and it is very difficult to prove the truth. Workers often feel unsupported and isolated whilst an investigation is taking place. Effective systems need to be set up so that a worker does receive the necessary support on a regular basis. The worker who is accused of abusing a client needs to be able talk about the situation (not just when they are being interviewed for investigative purposes) and how they are feeling. The manager should take responsibility for organizing this. However, sometimes this proves very difficult because the manager can become involved in the investigation. If there is no-one within the department who can support the worker (for example, a staff counsellor) then there is a need to find support outside the agency.

Whistleblowing is very topical at the moment and again a worker who 'grasses' on a colleague is often sent to coventry by other colleagues and life is made very difficult for him/her. In these situations a manager should listen to the worker in the first instance and then support them as much as s/he can. A manager should take responsibility for organizing regular support for the worker. The manager should also try to ensure that other team members behave professionally and do not make life difficult for that worker.

SOME EXERCISES FOR MANAGERS

I hope that managers will use the exercises in this book to develop and promote good practice in their teams. The following exercises are specifically for managers to help them in their own practice.

Suggested Reading

In order to manage cases of elder abuse managers need to be familiar with their department's policies and guidelines regarding abuse and to read more about supervision techniques. Also, a great deal can be learnt from what has happened in managing child abuse cases.

Atherton, J.S. (1986) *Professional Supervision in Group Care.* London: Tavistock.

Hawkins, P. and Shohet, R. (1989) *Supervision in the Helping Professions.* Buckingham: Open University Press.

Kadushin, A. (1976) *Supervision in Social Work.* New York: Columbia University Press.

Payne, C. and Scott, T. (1982) *Developing Supervision of Teams in Field and Residential Social Work.* London: National Institute for Social Work – Paper No 12.

Pritchard, J. (1995) *Good Practice in Supervision.* London: Jessica Kingsley.

Reder, P., Duncan, S. and Gray, M. (1993) *Beyond Blame – Child Abuse Tragedies Revisited.* London: Routledge.

BOUNDARIES OF CONFIDENTIALITY

Objective

To consider when the boundaries of confidentiality have to be broken

Participants

Exercise to be carried out in small groups

Equipment

Trainer to prepare handouts beforehand

Time

Groups to spend five minutes on each situation

Feedback

Task

Participants to discuss what they would do in their role as manager in these situations

Some Suggestions for Situations

One of your home helps has seen a neighbour take money from a client's side-board drawer. The home help talked to the client, who had *not* given permission for the neighbour to take the money. The home help has had suspicions about this neighbour before when money has disappeared. The client says she does not want any 'trouble or fuss'.

A home help reports to you that she knows that a district nurse has been colluding with a patient's wife by not giving enemas as prescribed. The wife says it is 'too messy and makes the house smell'. The home help overheard a conversation which confirmed her suspicions whilst she was in the kitchen making a cup of tea. She does not want the wife or district nurse to know she has reported what she heard.

A home help works with Mr Jeffries, who is severely disabled, having suffered several strokes. He has told the home help that he has huge financial problems because his daughter is taking most of his benefits and keeps drawing money out of his bank. Mr Jeffries now has rent arrears and is threatened with gas and electricity disconnections. He has confided in the home help and does not want her to tell anyone else.

A mentally sound 88-year-old woman has told a care assistant that her son regularly forced her to have sexual intercourse with him when she was living at home, even though she pleaded with him to stop. The client says she had to tell someone and says she is still scared of her son now. She does not want the care assistant to do anything but listen. The son visits his mother regularly in the home.

You are a manager in a residential unit. One of your care assistants tells you that she has found a lot of bruising on the body of Eli, who has come in for respite care. Eli, who is 65 years old and has a mental health problem, has admitted that his daughter in law hits him. He does not want anyone to know except the care assistant whom he trusts.

A residential worker reports that she knows a colleague is over medicating some residents and physically restraining others. She gives exact details and dates of incidents, but says she will not talk to anyone else about this and does not want it known that she has reported this to you. She refuses to make written statements and will not talk to the police.

DEVELOPING A STRATEGY

Objective

For a manager to think about a current problem s/he has in working with elder abuse and to develop a strategy to deal with it

Participant

To work individually

Equipment

Paper and pen

Time

20 minutes to work alone on one problem

20 minutes to discuss in pairs

Task

To think of a current problem relating to elder abuse (this can be anything from dealing with a worker who abused a client, a problematic case, not being able to get a worker to vent his/her feelings, a personal problem in dealing with an aspect of elder abuse). Write down the key issues which make it a problem. Develop a strategy to resolve the problem.

Feedback

Participants will feedback in pairs. Each will participant will have 10 minutes to talk about their problem and strategy, whilst the other participant will listen and make suggestions to improve the strategy.

ACTION PLANS

Objective

For a manager to develop an action plan to help his/her team develop and improve ways of working with elder abuse over the next three months

Participants

To work individually

Equipment

Paper pens

Envelopes

Diaries

Time

20 minutes to work on plan

20 minutes to feedback in pairs

Task

Participants need to reflect on how his/her team needs to develop in regard to working with elder abuse (think about current gaps in knowledge, experience). Each participant then needs to think about five things they would like to do in the next three months to promote team development. Handout 10.3 can be used for this exercise.

Feedback

Participants work in pairs to discuss their action plans.

After the exercise

The trainer gives each participant an envelope. Participants are asked to put their action plan in the envelope and write on the front 'Action Plan'. They are then asked to get their diaries and open it at the date three months ahead, where they will write 'Open Action Plan'.

Action Plan

for

....

(Name of team)

(A) Areas which need to be worked on

(B) Five tasks that the manager is going to undertake in the next three months

(1)

(2)

(3)

(4)

(5)

Signed.. Date:........................

11 Role Plays

This chapter includes role play situations which can be adapted to facilitate learning and the materials presented in Chapters 3 and 4. Role plays are a useful way of getting participants to find out whether they know what they are doing and whether they feel confident. Role plays make workers think about their own practice.

The trainer needs to do some preparation before using role play as an exercise. Decisions must be made about:

- what is the purpose of the role play
- will it run observed or unobserved
- can participants stop and start when things go wrong
- how long will it run for

Participants need to have their role defined on a card and preparation time is needed for them to think about how they are going to play the role. The objective of the exercise needs to be explained clearly as well as how feedback will be given.

HOME CARE STAFF

Role Play I

ROLE: HOME CARE ASSISTANT

You have been worried about Eunice for quite some time, because you are sure that her husband, Austin, has a drink problem and hits her. Eunice frequently has black eyes and bruises, but says 'she is getting clumsy' and is falling. You have found lots of whisky bottles hidden in peculiar places around the house. Eunice is a strong methodist and does not drink. Austin always goes bowling on a Wednesday, so today you are going to take the opportunity to tell Eunice you are worried about her and be honest with her about what you think is going on.

ROLE: EUNICE

You are married to Austin, who has a drink problem. You had a strong Methodist upbringing and have always hated drink in the house. Things have got worse recently and Austin hits you frequently. You still love him and are very loyal towards him. Your home care assistant has asked you about the injuries you have sustained, but you have always had good excuses and keep saying 'I am getting very clumsy in my old age'. Austin has gone to his bowls game today. You are alone in the house with the home care assistant.

HOME CARE STAFF

Role Play 2

ROLE: HOME CARE ASSISTANT

Today you are working with Olivia, who suffers from senile dementia. Olivia has disclosed that her brother, William, has been having sex with her. You are a bit confused yourself because Olivia also keeps talking about her father. In your mind you think she may be telling the truth about William, because over the past six months Olivia has had a lot of urinary infections and you have noticed nasty discharges on her knickers, which the GP has said is thrush. You are now going to try to get more detail from Olivia.

Role: OLIVIA

This morning you have disclosed to your home care assistant that your brother, William, has been having sex with you. You suffer from senile dementia, so your disclosure is hard to follow. One minute you are talking about William, the next minute you are talking about your father (who sexually abused you as a child). The home care assistant is now trying to find out more from you. The truth is that William has sexually abused you since he came to live with you five years ago after his wife died.

HOME CARE STAFF

Role Play 3

ROLE: HOME CARE ASSISTANT 1

Today you are working with another home care assistant. All morning she has seemed very agitated. She has been short tempered with clients and has also shouted at you. You have just asked her what is the matter and she has burst into tears.

ROLE: HOME CARE ASSISTANT 2

Today you are working with another home care assistant. All morning you have been short tempered with clients and you have shouted at your colleague. She has just asked you what is wrong and you have burst into tears. You are now going to confess that you have been taking money from clients. You have a gambling problem and cannot stop buying instant lottery tickets when you go shopping for clients. You have been taking £1 from each person's shopping to buy the tickets.

HOME CARE STAFF

Role Play 4

ROLE: HOME CARE ASSISTANT

Today you are going to talk to the son of Celia, Richard. Celia is your client; she is 73 years old and has severe arthritis. She is housebound apart from attending day centre twice a week. Celia has disclosed to you that Richard is not giving her the pension once he has cashed it. He handles all his mother's financial affairs. Celia is upset because he only allows her £5 per week 'spending money' which is meant to buy lunches at the day centre, her sweets and Women's Own magazine. Celia has developed an under-active thyroid and as a result of this has put on a lot of weight. She would like to buy some new clothes but Richard has told her it would be ridiculous at her age. Celia has asked you to talk to Richard 'discretely' about her needs.

ROLE: RICHARD, SON OF CELIA

Your mother is Celia, who is 73 years old. She has severe arthritis and is housebound apart from attending day centre twice a week. You handle all her financial affairs. You refuse to let her have her pension and only give her £5 per week to pay for her lunches at day centre, her sweets and Woman's Own magazine. Recently you have refused to buy new clothes for your mother (who is now suffering from an under-active thyroid gland and has put on a lot of weight) because you think it is ridiculous to waste money on clothes at her age. You believe the money is yours anyway and want to preserve your inheritance.

You are in fact using your mother's money for your own purposes. Your wife is very materialistic and is always wanting to buy things for the house. She also demands to go on holiday abroad twice a year. You are not highly paid, so money is a problem for you.

The home care assistant has asked to speak to you today.

HOME CARE STAFF

Role Play 5

ROLE: HOME CARE ASSISTANT

You have gone in to work with Carmel this morning. Carmel is severely disabled having suffered a stroke. She lives with Hannah, who was her daughter's best friend (her daughter died eight years ago). Hannah is single and works during the day. She moved in after Carmel had her stroke. You have noticed a decline in Carmel during the past year. She has become very thin and on occasions it seems she has not been washed. When you arrive this morning Carmel is crying.

ROLE: CARMEL

You are severely disabled having suffered a stroke. You live with Hannah, who was your daughter's best friend (your daughter died eight years ago). Hannah is single and works during the day. She moved in after you had your stroke. Hannah has been neglecting you. She does not feed you properly, as she says she is too tired to cook when she comes in and she does not like helping you to get washed, dressed or use the commode. She insists that you go to bed at 8.00 p.m. You find it difficult to say anything because she has offered to look after you and you have no-one else, but today it has all got too much for you and you are crying when the home care assistant arrives. You are going to tell her everything.

RESIDENTIAL STAFF

Role Play 6

ROLE: PRINCIPAL

You have been concerned about Miss Evergreen, who comes in for respite care, because she always has bruises on her back. Miss Evergreen lives with her nephew, Sebastian, whom you have asked to come in to speak to you today. You are going to ask him about the bruises.

ROLE: SEBASTIAN (NEPHEW OF MISS EVERGREEN)

You live with your aunt, Miss Evergreen, who goes in to a residential unit for regular respite care. The principal has asked you to come in to see her today.

Role Play 7

ROLE: CARE ASSISTANT

You walk into the lounge where you find Anthony Wareing, son of Doris Wareing, crying. Doris has been a permanent resident in your home for the past two months.

ROLE: ANTHONY WAREING (SON OF DORIS)

Your mother became a permanent resident in a private nursing home two months ago. You have had an incestuous relationship with her for the past 30 years, but she has refused to have sexual intercourse with you since she came into the home. She has rejected you again today. A care assistant finds you crying in the lounge. You say to her 'My mother doesn't want me anymore'.

RESIDENTIAL STAFF

Role Play 8

- -

ROLE: CARE ASSISTANT

> You and another care assistant are bathing Eleanor, who weighs eighteen stone and is dementing. Eleanor can be very difficult when being bathed, because she is scared of water. Today she is being very awkward and says she does not want to get into the bath. The other care assistant is getting very rattled. She starts shouting at Eleanor and eventually hits her very hard on her arms and her legs

- -

ROLE: CARE ASSISTANT

> You and another care assistant are bathing Eleanor, who weighs eighteen stone and is dementing. Eleanor can be very difficult when being bathed, because she is scared of water. Today she is being very awkward and says she does not want to get into the bath. You are getting very rattled. You have shouted at Eleanor and now you have just hit her very hard on her arms and her legs.

Role Play 9

- -

ROLE: CARE ASSISTANT

> Another care assistant has told you that she knows a colleague is stealing money from residents. She does not want to report it, but you think she should.

- -

ROLE: CARE ASSISTANT

> You have told another care assistant that you know a colleague is stealing money from residents. You do not want to get involved and have said that you will not report it. You are intimidated by the colleague who is abusing residents.

RESIDENTIAL STAFF

Role Play 10

ROLE: CARE ASSISTANT

> You are the keyworker for Samuel, who is a homosexual. He has talked to you openly about his sexuality and about his partner who died of AIDS three years ago. He has been very settled since coming to live in the home, but over the past month he has become withdrawn. He sits in the lounge all day and never wants to go to bed. Today you are going to try find out what is wrong.

ROLE: SAMUEL

> You have lived in this residential unit for the past three years; since your partner died of AIDS. You are very open about your sexuality and have talked a lot to your keyworker, whom you really like and trust. However, one of the male care assistants, who is also homosexual, has been touching you inappropriately when toiletting you and one night you woke up and found him lying on your bed. Recently you have been staying in the lounge and refusing to go to bed. Your keyworker is talking to you today.

DAY CENTRE STAFF

Role Play 11

- -

ROLE: DAY CENTRE WORKER

Mrs Kalinsky, aged 82 years, has arrived at day centre very distressed. She has indicated that she wants to talk to you in private.

- -

ROLE: MRS KALINSKY (AGE 82)

Your husband has always beaten you. You cannot run away like you used to do. Last night was worse than ever. Today you arrive at day centre very distressed. You have said you want to speak to one of the workers in private. You will tell the worker about the abuse and that you want to leave your husband now.

- -

DAY CENTRE STAFF

Role Play 12

ROLE: DAY CENTRE WORKER

> Mr and Mrs Hinchliff come to day centre together. They always present as a very loving couple. Mrs Hinchliff is severely disabled and can only get about in a wheelchair. Today Mrs Hinchliff has told you that her husband has a drink problem and that he becomes violent when he is drunk. He has hit her this morning and she is crying whilst talking to you. She says she cannot stand it anymore and wants you to talk to her husband.

ROLE: MR SHAW

> You attend the day centre with your wife, who is severely disabled and wheelchair bound. You are the primary carer. You have a drink problem, which you deny. You have always drunk heavily but now feel you need to drink more because of the stress you experience caring for your wife. You have hit your wife this morning. She has been crying whilst talking to the day centre worker, who is now going to talk to you.

DAY CENTRE STAFF

Role Play 13

ROLE: DAY CARE ASSISTANT

Frederick has been coming to the day centre for years now. He is a lovely man who gets on with everyone. However, during the past twelve months he has started to become forgetful. He misplaces things and forgets what day it is. He has said several times recently that money is going missing in his house.

ROLE: FREDERICK

You have been coming to the day centre for years now. During the past twelve months you have started to become forgetful. You misplace things and forget what day it is. Money is going missing in your house and you are convinced that it is one of the home care assistants who is taking it from under your mattress. You also think she is overcharging you for the shopping she does. This is really playing on your mind and you are going to talk to one of the day centre workers about it.

DAY CENTRE STAFF

Role Play 14

- -

ROLE: DAY CENTRE WORKER

Mr Khan has asked if he can talk to you today. You have no idea what about. Mr Khan lives with his wife who is terminally ill. He comes to day centre once week for a break.

- -

ROLE: MR KHAN

Your wife is terminally ill and you are finding it impossible to cope. You feel exhausted and unable to cope any longer. You cannot bear seeing your wife in so much pain. You have been over medicating her to help relieve the pain, but feel guilty about this. Last night you put a pillow over her head but then realized what you were doing. You want to talk to someone about how you feel. Your doctor and your sons are not sympathetic. They say it is your duty to carry on.

- -

DAY CENTRE STAFF

Role Play 15

- -

ROLE: DAY CENTRE WORKER

> One of the users, Mrs Lowe, says that she must talk to you about another user, Mrs Saunders, because she is very concerned about her.

- -

ROLE: MRS LOWE

> Another day centre user, Mrs Saunders, who is Afro Caribbean, has confided in you that her son has an addiction to crack, but is also dealing in drugs to finance his habit. Mrs Saunders is very frightened because her son becomes very violent towards her and she is also frightened of the people he brings into the house. She has confided in you because she had to tell someone. She made you promise not to tell anyone. You have been worried sick since she told you and now you are going to confide in the day centre worker whom you trust.

- -

© Jacki Pritchard, 1996

12 Case Studies

Case studies can be used in a variety of ways and it is up to the trainer to decide how the following material can best be adapted and used to suit the needs of course participants. However, I do have some suggestions for general use of the studies.

Brief information is given about the victim/and or abuser and the circumstances of the case. The way the cases are presented will raise many questions for the participants which should facilitate their learning. Participants can be asked to work in small groups to discuss the case in general, but also to answer the final questions on the information sheet.

During the group discussion, participants should think about:

o **Is this a case of elder abuse?**

o **Why does this constitute abuse?**

o **What should be done to help the victim/abuser?**

o **If you were involved in this case, how would you feel?**

✓

CASE STUDIES FOR HOME CARE STAFF

Case Study 1

SUBJECT: Ivy (age 65)

Ivy lives alone in a ground floor flat. She has learning difficulties and cannot read or write. A couple of years ago she suffered a stroke, so now she cannot walk very far and has to use a zimmer frame. The only time Ivy goes out is when she attends luncheon club twice a week.

Both a social worker and home care assistant have been involved with Ivy for quite some time. There have been concerns in the past when Ivy has said she has not got any money left. She has never said where the money has gone. Only on one occasion did she say that she had given some money to her 25 year old daughter, Tracey.

This weekend the police have been called out by a neighbour, who had heard Ivy shouting for help through the wall. When the neighbour went in she found Ivy crying and saying she was starving. It seems Tracey had come to visit and whilst Ivy was on the toilet she took all the money out of her mother's purse and left the flat. Ivy had not eaten for three days.

You are the home care assistant. You arrive at Ivy's flat on Monday morning to find the neighbour in with Ivy. They both tell you what has happened over the weekend and then Ivy tells you that it has happened before.

DISCUSS: **What would you want to find out from Ivy?**

What would you do next?

CASE STUDIES FOR HOME CARE STAFF

Case Study 2

SUBJECT: Isaac (age 70)

Isaac has lived with his partner, David, for the past 40 years. Isaac had a severe stroke five years ago, which has left him immobile and in fact he can do very little for himself. David is the sole carer, but it seems that he now resents the fact that he is tied down and cannot enjoy his retirement with Isaac as he expected to do.

You have become concerned that David may be neglecting Isaac both physically and emotionally. David is now going out more and frequently leaves Isaac on his own for long periods of time. David also invites friends round to the house and you have witnessed them making fun of Isaac.

Today you arrive at about 10.00 a.m. and Isaac tells you that David has been out all night. Isaac is very distressed because his catheter bag has not been changed and he is hungry.

DISCUSS: **What would you do first?**

What would you say to Isaac?

What would you do later on?

CASE STUDIES FOR HOME CARE STAFF

Case Study 3

SUBJECT: Lydia (age 92)

Lydia lives with her 52-year-old son Michael, who openly says that he hates his mother. Michael has always lived at home. He has rarely been employed, although he tells everyone that he is 'a genius'. He refers to his mother as being 'thick and stupid'.

Lydia is very confused. She is doubly incontinent, but Michael believes she deliberately urinates and defecates in her pants and on the bedclothes in order to spite him. Michael can be very bad tempered and frequently shouts at his mother.

When you bath Lydia she becomes very aggressive and does not like you to touch her. She often says things like 'Don't touch me you pervert' or 'I'm not a donkey you know'. She sometimes complains that she is 'itchy down below'.

Some days you cannot gain entry to the house and you worry what might be going on. Michael refuses all offers of help, including day centre, for his mother. Today you are washing some underwear for Lydia and you see blood on her knickers.

DISCUSS: **What are you thinking now?**

Would you discuss anything with Lydia?

What would you do next?

CASE STUDIES FOR HOME CARE STAFF

Case Study 4

SUBJECT: Raymond (age 85)

During the past year, Raymond has become confused and it seems the condition is becoming worse. However, he does have lucid moments when he talks very rationally to you. Raymond's wife died two years ago and he is now living with his son, Stanley, and his daughter in law, Vera (both of whom are in their early sixties).

Raymond suffered a stroke last year which has left him with restricted mobility, although he can walk with a zimmer frame. He does not go out any more and tends to spend most of his time in the front room, which Vera and Stanley have made into a bedsit for him. He complains to you that he is never allowed out and he misses going to the Legion.

You are concerned because Raymond has said some disturbing things to you recently. It is often difficult to understand what Raymond is referring to because he sometimes says 'They hurt me. Tell them to stop it' or 'She is trying to kill me. Please get me out of here'.

Raymond was captured in World War II and was imprisoned for a time in a concentration camp. He talks to you about being 'hurt', 'tortured' and 'threatened'. Sometimes you know he is definitely talking about the Germans, but at other times it seems he is talking about Vera and Stanley. Today when you visit, Raymond has a black eye and bruising on his right cheek. He tells you that Vera has hit him.

DISCUSS: **What would give you cause for concern in this case?**

How would you try to find out more from Raymond?

What questions would you ask to focus Raymond on time and people?

What would you do next?

CASE STUDIES FOR HOME CARE STAFF

Case Study 5

SUBJECT: Maud (age 89)

You have been involved with Maud for several years now. Maud has gradually become more confused and her social worker is now assessing whether she needs residential care. Maud has never married and all her relatives are dead. The only person who visits her is Cedric, who was her late brother's best friend.

You go into see Maud three times a day. You usually do your first visit around 8.30 a.m. On a few occasions when you have gone in earlier (usually when your other clients, whom you visit earlier, have gone into hospital or for respite care), you have found Cedric cooking breakfast. He has said that he has been passing by and called in. He has always emphasized that he is an early riser and likes to get out and about 'to make the most of the beautiful world around us'. Something about Cedric makes you feel very uncomfortable, but you cannot explain what it is exactly.

For the past month or so, you have become concerned about Maud. She's seems even more confused than usual and also very bad tempered (which is totally out of character) when you suggest helping her to wash and dress. Last week you found blood on Maud's nightdress. She could not explain how it had got there.

Today you go in at 8.30 a.m. as normal. You go up to Maud's bedroom; she is normally awake at this time. When you walk into the room you see Maud and Cedric asleep in bed.

DISCUSS: **What are your thoughts about this situation?**

What would you do next?

Case Study 6

SUBJECT: Albert (age 68)

Albert, who is aged 68, has been a resident in Holberry Grove for a year now. He has suffered one stroke, which affected his left arm; he is also a diabetic. He has always been considered a difficult man both by his family and staff in the home. This is because he is always moaning about what a miserable life he has had, but also because he makes nasty comments about people and often ridicules them. He swears at staff most days and on occasions has become physically aggressive. Staff have often complained to the principal of the unit, but she has said it is their job 'to get on with it'.

Last week a female resident, Elizabeth, was extremely upset and said 'it was all to do with Albert'. She would not say exactly what he had done and wanted it 'all forgotten'. She cried solidly for two days. Elizabeth is 80 years old and slightly forgetful. Her mobility is restricted having suffered two strokes; she uses a zimmer frame and a wheelchair when necessary. Another resident has told staff that Elizabeth is frightened of Albert. Today Albert is in a really bad mood. He threw his cereal bowl at a care assistant during breakfast and has been swearing at other residents. Later in the afternoon, another care assistant walked into one of the small 'quiet' lounges and saw Albert hit Elizabeth across the face.

DISCUSS: **What should happen now?**

Should something have been done before the current incident?

What are the key issues in this case?

Case Study 7

SUBJECT: Sabrina (age 78)

Sabrina has been a resident in Alderly Lodge since her husband died three years ago. She has always been a friendly woman and likes to be involved with staff and other residents. However, during the past year she has become slightly confused; some days she is perfectly lucid but on other days she is completely muddled.

Some staff now see Sabrina as 'a problem', because she has started to have vivid nightmares. She dreams about how her husband forced her to have sex with him. Sabrina did talk to her keyworker about this a few months after she came into the unit, but did not want to discuss it after the initial disclosure. She had said that her husband had been extremely violent throughout the marriage and that he demanded 'his conjugal rights too often and even when I was ill'.

Sabrina's nightmares are now occurring every night. During the day she constantly walks around the unit crying and telling staff she wants to talk about her nightmares. Staff discussed the situation in a meeting and agreed that with staff shortages they just have not got the time to keep listening and talking to Sabrina. The GP was contacted and staff told him they thought Sabrina needed 'calming down'. The GP prescribed her medication which made her very drowsy through the day.

DISCUSS: **What are Sabrina's needs?**

What help/support does Sabrina need?

Were staff correct in their assessment?

What would you have done differently?

CASE STUDIES FOR RESIDENTIAL AND DAY CARE STAFF

Case Study 8

SUBJECT: Gordon (age 77)

Gordon has suffered a stroke and consequently his personality has changed a great deal. His wife, Joyce, finds it very difficult to cope. Gordon has started to have regular respite care. Whenever he comes in for a stay he always seems sluggish and his mobility is very poor.

Everyone who is involved with Gordon and Joyce are voicing their concerns. The home helps and district nurse are noticing that Joyce often has black eyes and bruises on her face. Joyce does talk about the changes in her husband; she says he used to be a very a loving person. She eventually admits that Gordon does hit her. Joyce has very poor eyesight and often cannot get out of the way quick enough when Gordon hits her or throws objects at her. The social worker is counselling Joyce about her situation.

You are a member of staff working in the residential unit where Gordon has respite care. Staff have discussed the possibility that Gordon is being over-medicated, because by the end of each stay he is bright and alert, but when he returns for his next stay in six weeks time he is always drowsy again. The Principal has reported this to the social worker, but she has refused to carry out an investigation.

DISCUSS: **What are the key issues in the case?**

What should the residential staff do to pursue their concerns?

CASE STUDIES FOR RESIDENTIAL AND DAY CARE STAFF

Case Study 9

SUBJECT: Mrs Delia Burrows (age 69)

Mrs Delia Burrows is an Afro-Caribbean woman who attends a local authority day centre two days a week. She is the only black user in the centre. This was discussed with her before she was allocated a place there and she said it would not be a problem for her. Mrs Burrows has suffered several strokes and does not have use of her left arm. Her husband is the sole carer for her and she acknowledges that he needs a rest, so was happy to come to the day centre.

Mrs Burrows is a very quiet and private woman, but enjoys getting involved in the centre's activities. However, over the past month she has become upset on several occasions and one day shouted at one of the day centre staff. When another day centre worker asked Mrs Burrows if anything was wrong she confided that the male worker upsets her. She said he always calls her Delia when she had asked to be called Mrs Burrows; she feels this is showing a lack of respect. Also, he had been touching her inappropriately. Mrs Burrows talked about him being 'over familiar', 'touching my bottom' and 'brushing against me'. The day centre worker who heard the disclosure laughed and told Delia 'Don't be so silly. He does that to all us women. It doesn't mean anything'.

DISCUSS: Is this a case of abuse?

What should the day centre worker have done when Mrs Burrows disclosed to her?

What would you have said to Mrs Burrows if she had told you about these incidents?

Case Study 10

SUBJECTS: Mr and Mrs Bridges (both in their sixties)

Mr and Mrs Bridges come to day centre once a week. They were both in a car crash five years ago; Mrs Bridges was driving. Mrs Bridges is severely disabled as a result of the crash. Mr Bridges is not as active as he used to be and resents the fact that he cannot spend his retirement as he had planned to do (taking long walks in the country, working on his allotment etc). He has to spend most of his time caring for his wife.

Mrs Bridges has confided in you that her husband has started to drink quite heavily and is often very bad tempered with her. He has hit her once, but she did not want you to do anything about it.

During the past few weeks Mr Bridges has started making derogatory comments to his wife in front of other day centre users. He ridicules her and says 'she is good for nothing'.

Today when the couple arrive at the day centre Mrs Bridges has two black eyes and is very weepy.

DISCUSS: **What would you do when you see Mrs Bridges today?**

What sort of questions would you ask her?

Would you say anything to Mr Bridges?

What should you have done on previous occasions when Mr Bridges has verbally abused his wife in front of other day centre users?

Keeping Healthy

By the end of this book you will know more about:

- How to have a healthy and balanced diet.

- How your heart works and how it is affected by exercise.

- How tobacco, alcohol and other drugs can harm your body.

- How too much Sun can harm your body.

You will:

- Find and measure your pulse.

- Plan and carry out an investigation and know the importance of taking repeat readings.

- Present results in bar charts and line graphs.

To stay healthy we need a balanced and varied diet.

Task 1 — True or false?

Read and copy the sentences below.

Write **T** by those you think are true and **F** by those you think are false.

1 Chocolate bars are the best food for a healthy diet.

2 Apples give us lots of energy to be active.

3 Milk contains most things we need to keep healthy, to grow and to be active.

4 Only meat contains foods to help us grow.

5 Water is good for giving us energy to be active.

6 Fish is a food that helps us grow.

7 Bread is a food that mostly helps us grow.

8 Chips should be eaten everyday to he us to be active.

9 Jacket potatoes are healthier for us than crisps.

10 Too much starch can make us fat.

11 Fresh fruit and vegetables are foods w need to keep healthy.

Share your answers with others in you group. Do they agree or disagree with your answers?

Task 2 — Know your foods

To eat wisely and healthily, we need to know about food. There are hundreds of kinds of foods, so we sort them into groups. The groups are based on what the foods do in our bodies. Some foods provide materials needed for healthy growth. Others provide energy.

Read the Fact File.

Copy and complete the table.

Food type	Source	Needed for
	Bread, pasta, rice	Energy
Fats		
	Meat, beans and lentils, dairy products	
Fibre		
		Making and keeping healthy bones and teeth

Fact File **Food groups**

Carbohydrates. These include cereals, bread, pasta, starchy vegetables and sugars. They help us to be active and they give us energy.

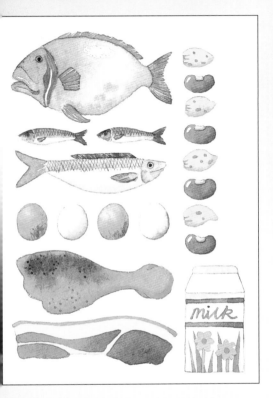

Proteins. These are found in foods such as lentils, some types of beans, meat, eggs, chicken, fish, nuts and dairy products. Proteins are important for building all parts of the body, including muscles and bones. They are essential for growth. Even when we stop growing, proteins are needed to replace or repair worn out parts.

Fats. These are found in dairy foods, some meats, margarine, and vegetable and fish oils. They are an important store of energy. If you eat too many fatty foods they can make you overweight and unhealthy.

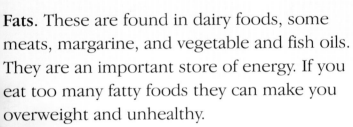

Fibre and vitamins. We get these from cereals, fruit and vegetables. You should eat plenty of these foods every day as they help to keep us healthy. Lack of fibre in the diet when young may cause problems of the digestive system and heart later in life. Fruit and vegetables also contain very small amounts of substances called vitamins – all important for healthy bones and teeth, good night vision and healthy blood.

(3)

Fact File   Diet and health

You would not live for very long if you had a diet of only sugar, protein and water. Your body also needs small amounts of **vitamins** to stay healthy.

One of these, **vitamin C**, is found in some fruits and vegetables – especially **citrus fruits** such as lemons, limes and oranges. It is also put into bread and cereals. Your body needs a small amount of vitamin C every day to stay healthy.

If you don't get enough vitamin C in your diet you may get a condition known as **scurvy**. Signs of scurvy are:

• a swollen body causing painful movements

• split and bleeding gums

• a swollen tongue and throat.

Many people used to die of scurvy because it stopped them eating and drinking.

Hundreds of sailors in the sixteenth and seventeenth centuries died of scurvy at sea because there was little vitamin C in their normal diet – mostly dry biscuits, salty meat and water. They often ate no fresh fruit or vegetables for weeks at a time.

When British explorer Captain James Cook set off on a voyage between 1772 and 1775, he made sure he sailed with a good supply of pickled cabbage, cress and orange juice. All these contain vitamin C. Whenever possible he also took on board fresh fruits. Because his crew had plenty of vitamin C in their diet they remained fit and healthy and there was no scurvy on board.

Fresh supplies for
Captain Cook

The link between diet and health

Read the Fact File.

Ship's Log march 1769
We headed south in the company of several hundred porpoises.
The scurvy has struck once more and today we buried two more able seamen and a plant scientist

Imagine that you are a sailor on board Captain Cook's ship before 1772.

Write in the ship's log on Task Sheet 1 describing the effects of scurvy on the crew.

Imagine that you are on board Captain Cook's ship after 1775.

Write in the ship's log on Task Sheet 1 describing how the ship stopped at an island to collect fresh food and explaining what effect this had on the crew's health.

Words to learn and use:
carbohydrate
citrus fruits
fats
fibre
protein
scurvy
vitamins

Eat well, eat wisely, keep healthy!

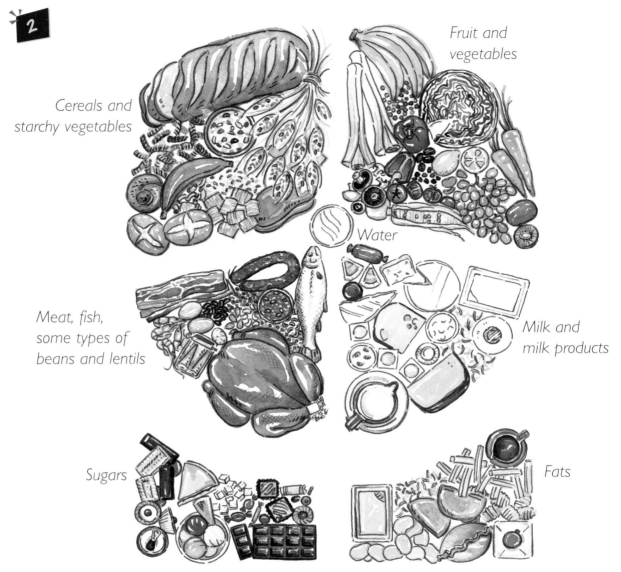

Cereals and starchy vegetables

Fruit and vegetables

Water

Meat, fish, some types of beans and lentils

Milk and milk products

Sugars

Fats

⭐ Look at the picture. It shows foods that make up the 'Wheel of healthy eating'. You should eat some foods from each section of the wheel each day. You can eat fats and sugars outside the wheel but in smaller amounts than other foods if you want to remain healthy.

⭐ In groups, research different diets, menus and information about food and healthy eating. You could choose from these:

- menus for school meals

- food to take on an expedition to the Antarctic

- food to take on an expedition across a desert

- food to make a school tuck shop more healthy.

⭐ Create a table showing the protein, carbohydrate, fat, fibre and vitamins in the different foods in your chosen diet.

⭐ Use Task Sheet 2 to help you.

⭐ Make a class display of your findings.

We need exercise to stay healthy and maintain our muscles.

How did you exercise yesterday?

You use muscles whenever you move, for example, when smiling, chewing, blinking or running.

Whether resting or exercising you use some of the 600 or so muscles in your body.

Think about how you used your muscles yesterday.

Divide the hours of the day into time spent exercising and time spent not exercising.

Make a bar chart of your findings. Use a framework like this to draw your bar chart.

Did you spend time watching TV, working on a computer, reading, riding in a car, bus or train? Did you spend time walking, playing ball games or playground games, riding a bicycle, dancing or doing P.E.?

Complete Task Sheet 3 to record what you did yesterday.

How much exercise and rest I have in a day

time (hours)

exercising   not exercising

Use your bar chart and completed Task Sheet to answer these questions:

Did you spend more time exercising or not exercising?

How much time did you spend on each?

Which kind of exercise did you do most of?

How did you take most of your rest?

Do you think that you get enough exercise? Explain why? (You should try to exercise hard for about an hour a day.)

Task
6

Exercise and health

Muscles need to work hard to keep healthy. When we exercise energetica[lly] we feel hotter and breathe faster. Wh[y] do you think we feel like this?

During exercise our muscles need mo[re] energy-giving foods, such as sugars. Blood carries this food and oxygen to [all] parts of our bodies and especially to muscles during exercise.
Muscles use this food and oxygen to release the energy they need to pull bones to make them move.

Your heart muscle is very important. I[t] works all the time – and even harder during exercise – to pump blood to t[he] muscles joined to the skeleton.
The harder we exercise, the more foo[d] and oxygen our muscles need. Some [of] that food is also changed into heat so we feel hotter and sweat more.

Design a 'Keeping Healthy' leaflet advertising how and why we should exercise.

The heart is a muscle that pumps blood around the body. The heart and lungs are protected by the ribs.

The heart

- The muscle in the walls of your heart contracts regularly.

- As your heart muscle contracts it pumps blood around your body and to your lungs.

- Your heart is in the middle of your chest. It is protected by your ribs. Your ribs also protect your lungs.

- Because the left side of your heart is bigger than the right, it feels as though your heart is on the left side.

- Your heart has four **chambers** – a right and left **atrium** and a right and left **ventricle**.

- Your heart is about the size of a clenched fist.

- The right-hand side of your heart is separate from the left-hand side.

- The right-hand side receives blood that carries carbon dioxide from your body. It then pumps this to your lungs.

- The left-hand side of your heart receives blood that has travelled from your lungs carrying oxygen. It then pumps this blood around your body.

- Blood leaves the heart in **arteries**. Arteries are tubes with thick walls.

- Blood returns to the heart in **veins**. Veins are tubes with thin walls.

- Arteries and veins are called blood vessels.

- Each beat of the left ventricle of your heart can be felt as a pulse where an artery passes over a bone, for example in your wrist.

- Your heart beats about 70 times a minute when you are resting.

- When resting, it takes 6 seconds for blood to be pumped to your brain and back to your heart.

Find out about your heart

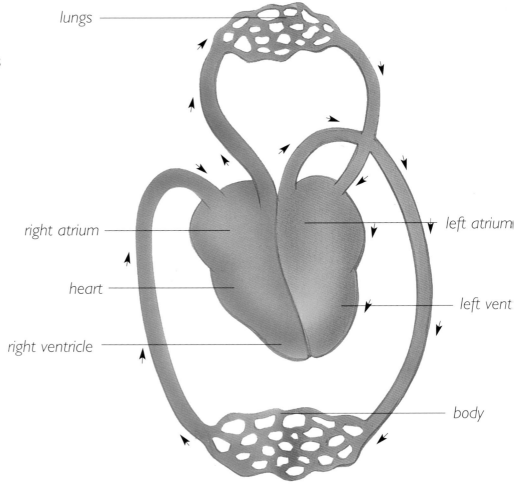

lungs

How blood moves
around the body

right atrium

heart

right ventricle

left atrium

left vent

body

When you draw the heart, you imagine
that you are looking at somebody from
the front. So the left atrium and left
ventricle are on their left side but on your
right side!

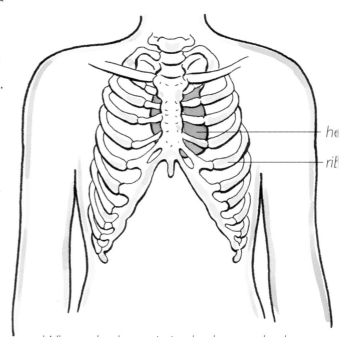

he

rib

⚝ Research using CD-ROMs, books and the
Internet to find out more about the heart.

⚝ Then:

• make up a true/false quiz about
the heart

OR

• use a balloon pump to explain how the
heart pumps blood around the body

OR

• prepare notes and diagrams to give a
short talk about the heart to the class.

Where the heart is in the human body

Blood vessels carry blood around the body.

Heart hopscotch

The heart pumps blood to all parts of the body. Every living part of the body makes carbon dioxide which must be breathed out of the lungs into the air if we are to stay alive. In this game, you are the blood carrying oxygen and carbon dioxide.

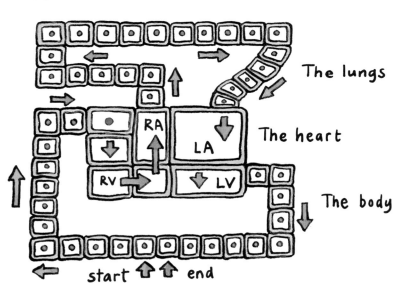

The lungs

The heart

The body

start ⬆ ⬆ end

Words to learn and use:
blood vessel
heart
muscles

How to play heart hopscotch in the playground:

Use blue counters for carbon dioxide.
Use red counters for oxygen.

Ask your teacher to draw a large heart and lungs on the playground surface like the one in the picture.

Put a blue counter in all the body squares. These are carbon dioxide made by the body.

Put red counters on the squares of the lungs. These are for vital oxygen.

Take five red counters and go to start.

Throw a bean bag into a square then hop to the bean bag square.

Put down a red counter in the square you land on and if there's a blue counter, pick it up. You are swapping oxygen for carbon dioxide.

7   Throw the bean bag again and continue to swap counters as you 'circulate' round the body. When you reach the lungs leave your blue (carbon dioxide) counters and pick up the red ones.

8   Hop back to the heart and into the body. Take it in turns to circulate.

9   Some of your group should replace the blue counters in the body squares and red counters in the lung squares as you go around the system.

✵   Hopping exercises the heart as well as the body. Count your pulse rate before and after hopping. When is it fastest? Why?

How to find and measure the pulse and take repeat readin

Scientific Enquiry
Pulse rates

Each time your heart beats, blood is pushed through arteries and veins. We can feel this 'push' of blood in arteries that pass over bones. Two places where you can feel your pulse with your fingertips (not your thumb) are the:

- temple of your forehead
- part of the wrist which is in line with the thumb.

Each pulse is caused by one beat of the heart.

Practise finding your pulse. What does it feel like?

Try finding a partner's pulse. Is it like yours?

Your pulse rate is the number of beats of your heart in one minute. Pulses can vary even for the same person so we measure them several times to get similar readings and find the middle reading.

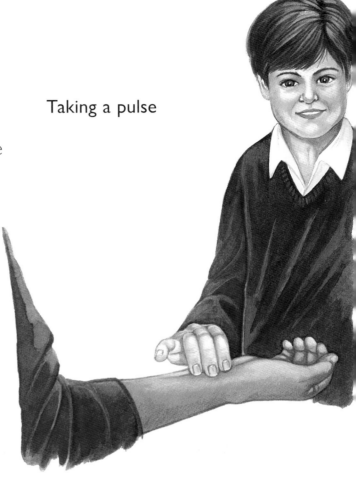

Taking a pulse

Carry out an experiment to find your pulse at rest.

1 Make a table for your results before you start, or set up a spreadsheet on the computer.

2 Find your pulse rate three times for three separate minutes.

3 Find your typical resting pulse rate.

Did your pulse vary or was it similar each time? Did your repeat readings give better results? Explain why.

you need:

- table for your results
- timer or clock that measures in seconds

Pulse rate (beats per minute)				
Name	1st try	2nd try	3rd try	Middle reading
Jon				

Sharing class results on resting pulse rates

Class 5 have found their typical pulse rates.

Name	Resting pulse rate
Jon	62
Suad	62
Jane	65
Parveen	67
Andrew	67
James	67
Tom	68
Susan	68
Gary	68
Dave	68
Anne	71
Megan	71

They decided to organise their pulse rates into three groups:

Group	No. of children
Pulse rate from 60 to 64	2
Pulse rate from 65 to 69	7
Pulse rate from 70 to 74	2

These groupings helped the children to draw a bar chart.

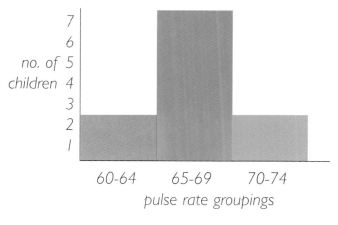

Typical pulse rates in Class 5

no. of children / pulse rate groupings (60-64, 65-69, 70-74)

Make your own class table of resting pulse rates. Use a large sheet of paper or computer spreadsheet to record your results.

As a class, order the results starting from the lowest pulse rate to the highest. With help from your teacher, group the results, like Class 5 did.

Draw a bar chart to show your results.

Using your bar chart, answer these questions:

1 Which was the most common range for pulse rates for the whole class?

2 How many groupings did you use?

3 What were the pulse rates of the lowest group?

4 Does your grouping of pulse rates give a good picture of pulse rates in your class? Explain why.

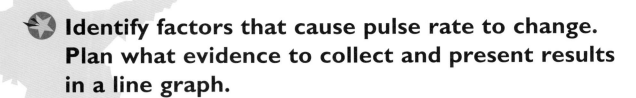

Identify factors that cause pulse rate to change. Plan what evidence to collect and present results in a line graph.

Scientific Enquiry

How does the time you exercise affect your pulse rate?

4

☆ Use the planning board on Task Sheet 4 to plan and carry out an investigation into how exercise affects pulse rate. As you plan think about these things:

- What sort of exercise you will do.

- Will you keep to one sort of exercise?

- Will you share your results with the class before drawing a graph?

⚠ *Check with your teacher that you are fit before you begin exercising. This is not a test of stamina or strength.*

☆ Draw a graph like this one. You could use a computer.

How the time spent exercising affects pulse rate.

pulse rate

length of exercise (minutes)

☆ What do your results tell you? Could you improve your enquiry? If so, how?

Exercise and fitness

A fit person has a heart that adapts quickly to changes in exercise or activity.

Helen is a fit person. Her normal pulse rate when resting is 64 beats per minute. Look at the line graph of Helen's pulse rate after exercise.

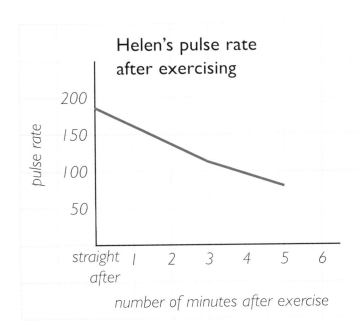

Helen's pulse rate after exercising

pulse rate

200

150

100

50

straight after | 1 | 2 | 3 | 4 | 5 | 6

number of minutes after exercise

Answer these questions.

1 What do you think Helen did to collect her data?

2 When was her pulse rate lowest? Why?

3 When was her pulse rate highest? Why?

4 How could you use the graph to find out how long it took for Helen's pulse rate to return to normal after exercise? Explain how you did it.

5 Why does pulse rate fall after exercise?

Words to learn and use:
activity
circulate
pulse
pulse rate
rest

Fact File
Health can be affected by different things

Your body can be harmed if it is not cared for properly.

You can become ill if harmful things get into your body.

Harmful things can affect your body:

- when you breathe
- when you eat and drink
- through your skin.

Tobacco smoke, too much alcohol, dirty air and other gases, and too much ultra-violet light are some things that can make you ill and cause disease.

Dirty air can make us ill

You need to know about these things so that you can protect your body from harm.

Fact File
Smoking

A health visitor came to Duncan's school. Here are her answers to Duncan's questions about smoking.

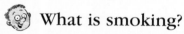 **What is smoking?**

It is when tobacco is burned to produce smoke which can be breathed into our lungs. Some parts of the smoke breathed into the lungs stay in the body.

What do people smoke?

Cigarettes, cigars, and pipe tobacco.

What is in smoke?

Mostly **carbon monoxide gas, nicotine** and **tar**.

What can these things do to us?

Carbon monoxide is poisonous. It takes the place of vital oxygen so that the heart and lungs have to work harder.

So what is nicotine?

Nicotine is a drug that makes the heart beat faster. It harms the heart, blood vessels and the nervous system. Nicotine makes people want to keep smoking – it is addictive. Nicotine also makes teeth and fingers yellow and smelly.

What makes smokers cough?

Tar, which is black and sticky. It coats the lungs, making it harder for oxygen to enter the blood.

Tobacco, alcohol and other drugs can be harmful and affect the way the body functions.

Smoking and health

5

Read the Fact File about smoking on page 16.

Complete this table.
Use Task Sheet 5 to help you.

Material in smoke	What it is like	What it does to the body
		Stops blood carrying oxygen
Nicotine		
	Black and sticky	

you will need:

- clear plastic bottle
- clear plastic tube
- different types of cigarettes – high tar and low tar
- Plasticine
- cotton wool
- timer

A smoke testing machine

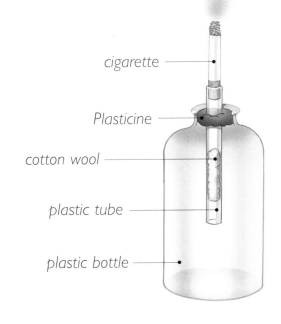

cigarette

Plasticine

cotton wool

plastic tube

plastic bottle

Task 14

Scientific Enquiry

What is in cigarette smoke?

You can use a testing machine to find out how much tar different brands of cigarettes contain.

✸ With your teacher, make a testing machine like the one in the picture.

✸ Design a table for your results.

✸ See how long each type of cigarette burns.

✸ Write down the results in your table.

✸ The tar will collect on the cotton wool – this is like the lungs. What does the cotton wool look like? What would your lungs look like if you smoked?

⚠ *This must only be done out of doors and by your teacher.*

Medicines are drugs but not all drugs are medicines.

To smoke or not to smoke?
....

Do you think you will smoke when you grow up?

★ Use Task Sheet 6 to write down some reasons for smoking and some reasons against smoking.

★ Use Task Sheet 7 to record the number of people in your class who say they will smoke and the number of people who say they will not smoke.

★ Use this information to make a poster to inform people about the effects of smoking.

Most smokers would like to stop smoking

Drugs and medicines

Drugs are substances which can change how your body works. Medicines are drugs that can often help to cure us when we are ill. For some medicines we have to go to the doctor but some can be bought from a pharmacy or shop. Some medicines may have unpleasant side effects. They may taste unpleasant or make us feel ill even when we follow the instructions for taking them, but over time they can help us get better.

Some drugs, such as tea, coffee and cola, we use safely everyday, but some drugs are illegal. It is against the law to use them. These are drugs that affect what we do and often cause death or serious illness.

Everyday drugs

Caffeine drinks

Look at the pictures.
Some everyday things such as coffee, tea and cola contain **caffeine**.
Caffeine is a drug.
It makes the heart beat faster and makes people feel less sleepy.
Nicotine is also a drug that acts like caffeine.

Alcohol is a drug that can affect people in different ways.

These are some of the ways that alcohol can affect people:

it can make them argue

it can make them do things more slowly

it makes them unsafe to drive a car.

Copy and complete this table.

Everyday product	Drug it contains	How it is taken	How it affects our bodies and behaviour
Wine	Alcohol		
Coffee			
Tea	Caffeine		
Beer			
Cigarette	Nicotine		

Fact File

Sunbathing

The Sun helps us to make vitamin D in our skin, which we use to make healthy teeth and bones.

Too much sunbathing can be harmful because it causes changes to happen in the skin.

This can cause a disease called skin cancer.

Protect your skin with high factor sun cream

Task 17 — Safe sunbathing

 8,9,10

 Read the play on Task Sheets 8 and 9

Complete Task Sheet 10.

Task 18 — Safe sun care

Choose one of the following:

1 Design a leaflet or make a poster on safe sunbathing.
Use CD-ROMs and the Internet to help you and use the information you collected on Task Sheet 10.

OR

2 Make up a rhyme about being in hot and sunny weather.

Present your work to the rest of the class.

Which was the best way of giving the message about safe sunbathing? Why?

Checkpoint 1

Healthy exercise

Muscles are used for every movement of your body, including activities such as swimming, running, jogging and skipping.

Remember:

Muscles move bones.

Muscles are attached to bones and work in pairs.

When one muscle shortens or tightens, the opposite one is relaxed, or stretched.

It is important to warm muscles with gentle exercise, such as stretching, before any activity, and to cool down at the end of an activity.

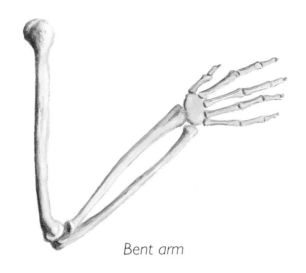

Bent arm

Review your work so far on exercising for keeping healthy.

Think of one form of exercise that you are interested in and design an illustrated leaflet explaining:

- what the exercise is

- which muscles are used

- how to warm up and cool down before and after the exercise

- how the heart beat and pulse rate get faster during the exercise and why this needs to happen.

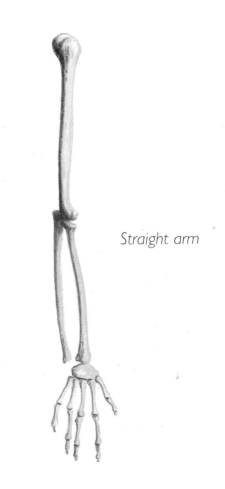

Straight arm

Checkpoint 2

Being healthy

✸ Design a leaflet or poster showing how alcohol or tobacco affects health. You could use the Internet to get more information and pictures.

✸ Develop some of the work you have done into a health magazine. You could use a computer to prepare articles, leaflets and posters to inform others about how to keep healthy. You could add some quizzes, word searches and puzzles to make your magazine fun as well as useful.

Summary

Which of these do you know and which can you do?

- I know that to stay healthy we need a balanced and varied diet.
- I know that we need exercise to stay healthy and maintain our muscles.
- I know that exercise makes muscles and the heart work harder.
- I know that the heart is a muscle that pumps blood around the body.
- I know that the heart and lungs are protected by the ribs.
- I know that blood vessels carry blood around the body.
- I know how to find and measure the pulse and take repeat readings.
- I can plan and carry out an investigation and use results to draw line graphs.
- I can identify factors that cause pulse rate to change.
- I can plan what evidence to collect and present results in a line graph.
- I know that tobacco, alcohol and other drugs can be harmful and affect the way the body functions.
- I know that medicines are drugs but not all drugs are medicines.

Complete your **Science Log** to show how well you know these and how well you can do them. Circle a face for each statement.

Glossary

arteries – thick walled tubes in the body that carry blood containing oxygen from your heart.

balanced diet – a mixture of different foods (fats, proteins, carbohydrate, fibre, sugars, minerals and vitamins) which keep the body healthy.

drugs – substances that cause changes to parts of the body. Medicines are drugs. Some drugs are harmful.

heart – a muscular pump that circulates blood around the body.

medicine – a drug that is often prescribed by a doctor to prevent or cure illness.

muscles – parts of the body that move bones.

pulse – where the regular beating of the heart can be felt.

pulse rate – the number of beats your heart makes in a minute.

starch – a carbohydrate found in plants that forms part of a healthy diet.

sugars – carbohydrates found in many plants. Some are used to sweeten foods.

veins – thin walled tubes that carry blood to your heart.

vitamins – substances found in food that are needed in small amounts to keep healthy.

carbohydrate

medicine